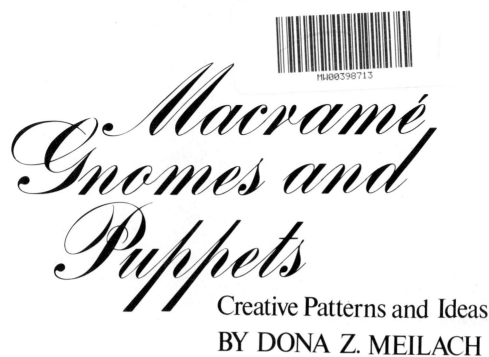

Macramé, Gnomes and Puppets

Creative Patterns and Ideas
BY DONA Z. MEILACH

CROWN PUBLISHERS, INC.   NEW YORK

MACRAMÉ: CREATIVE DESIGN IN KNOTTING
MACRAMÉ ACCESSORIES
PLANT HANGERS

ALSO:

FIBERS AND FABRICS

BASKETRY TODAY WITH MATERIALS FROM NATURE
    with Dee Menagh
CONTEMPORARY BATIK AND TIE DYE
CONTEMPORARY LEATHER
CREATING ART FROM FIBERS AND FABRICS
CREATIVE STITCHERY
    with Lee Erlin Snow
EXOTIC NEEDLEWORK WITH ETHNIC PATTERNS
    with Dee Menagh
MAKING CONTEMPORARY RUGS AND WALL HANGINGS
A MODERN APPROACH TO BASKETRY WITH FIBERS AND GRASSES
SOFT SCULPTURE AND OTHER SOFT ART FORMS
WEAVING OFF-LOOM
    with Lee Erlin Snow

CERAMIC-TILE

TILE DECORATING WITH GEMMA

SCULPTURE

CONTEMPORARY ART WITH WOOD
CONTEMPORARY STONE SCULPTURE
CREATING ART WITH BREAD DOUGH
CREATING MODERN FURNITURE
CREATING SMALL WOOD OBJECTS AS FUNCTIONAL SCULPTURE
CREATING WITH PLASTER

CREATIVE CARVING
DECORATIVE AND SCULPTURAL IRONWORK
DIRECT METAL SCULPTURE
    with Donald Seiden
SCULPTURE CASTING
    with Dennis Kowal
SOFT SCULPTURE AND OTHER SOFT ART FORMS

COLLAGE-PAPER

ACCENT ON CRAFTS
BOX ART: ASSEMBLAGE AND CONSTRUCTION
COLLAGE AND ASSEMBLAGE
    with Elvie Ten Hoor
COLLAGE AND FOUND ART
    with Elvie Ten Hoor
CREATING ART FROM ANYTHING
PAPERCRAFT
PAPIER-MÂCHÉ ARTISTRY
PRINTMAKING

DESIGN

THE ARTIST'S EYE
HOW TO CREATE YOUR OWN DESIGNS
    with Jay and Bill Hinz

ALSO:

THE ART OF BELLY DANCING
    with Dahlena
JAZZERCISE
    with Judi Missett
HOMEMADE LIQUEURS
    with Mel Meilach
HOW TO RELIEVE YOUR ACHING BACK

Inquiries should be addressed to Crown Publishers, Inc., One Park
Avenue, New York, New York 10016

Printed in the United States of America

Published simultaneously in Canada by General Publishing Company Limited

Library of Congress Cataloging in Publication Data

Meilach, Dona Z
Macramé gnomes and puppets.

Includes index.
1. Macramé. 2. Puppet making. 3. Soft sculpture. I. Title. II. Title: Gnomes and puppets:
creative patterns and ideas.
TT840.M42   745.59′22   79-20623
ISBN: 0-517-54010X

10 9 8 7 6 5 4 3 2 1

First edition

Contents

Acknowledgments

It was so much fun working with the artists who developed the ingenious variety of puppets and gnomes using macramé. None had ever tackled macramé in this same three-dimensional approach before. Each considered the assignment a challenge. Some were so intrigued by the potential that it led them into a completely new aspect of macramé activity.

I want to thank Mary Baughn, Kathy Browne, Pattie Frazer, Tina Johnson-Depuy, and Bob West for their inspired creations and for their willingness to share. I wish space allowed me to use all the pieces that were submitted for the book.

Thanks also, to my husband, Mel Meilach, for his help with the photography; to Rick Geary for his drawings of the macramé knots and construction details of the figures; to Allen Meilach for his interpretation of faces and bodies.

I appreciate the patience required to help decipher the instructions from hand-written analysis to final typewritten drafts by Collette Russell and Penny McBride. I want to extend my sincere appreciation to the macramé knotters who checked the instructions by re-creating new pieces from them: Jill Saens, Dora Dilson, and Susan Grayson.

Finally, my continuing gratitude to my editor, Brandt Aymar, who hesitates to question the validity of book ideas that I propose when the contents are only a vision in my head and nothing I can put to paper. His confidence is one of the magical ingredients that make the long, tedious, lonely hours of authorship worthwhile.

Dona Z. Meilach

Carlsbad, California
January 1980

Preface

When the idea for this book occurred to me, I decided the best way to evolve a grandiose scheme was to ask several crafts-people to create gnomes and puppets using their own imaginations and visual conceptions of such creatures. The beings that resulted inhabited my studio for months until they seemed like members of the family with personalities all their own. Returning them to their rightful owners was like sending a grandchild home to its parents.

Each artist sent along notes of the procedures used but, in addition, it took hours of analysis to determine how each figure evolved, amounts of cords used, and the best procedures for accomplishing the same results. The instructions offered are as accurate as possible. Each project was tested to create another figure from the instructions with the intention that a newcomer to macramé be able to follow the procedures.

Some of the instructions may appear lengthy, in print, but don't let that faze you. Gather your materials and dig in; if you find yourself going slightly astray, improvise. There is *no one way* to re-create each figure. A few more knots more or less will not affect the scheme of things. At worst, your puppet may be slightly fatter or thinner, taller or shorter. If it's completely different, then you've created your own version . . . and that's perfectly O.K.!

For color combinations, refer to the color section of the book. Do not hesitate to change colors in keeping with your tastes and the materials available. Puppet sizes given can be purposely adjusted for your own staging or decorative reasons to make them larger or smaller by altering the materials used or the length of the knotting. A change of character in puppetry can be achieved by accentuating any of the body proportions and the facial features just as a caricaturist emphasizes features in a drawing.

5

1. Why Macramé Puppets and Gnomes?

Puppets have been around for centuries. There are references that "string pullers" or operators of puppet shows existed in the Greek culture about 300 B.C. Marionettes and shadow puppets have a history in the theater and religious productions of ancient Rome and the Middle Ages. Puppets of varying forms existed in Asia and were well known in Europe during the Renaissance. In the 1800s the Punch and Judy shows of England were a slice-of-life type of theater. Johann Wolfgang Goethe, the great German poet, received a puppet theater on his twelfth birthday in 1761 and wrote his own plays for it.

With puppetry dating so far back, can there be something new? The answer is a resounding yes. It has been proven in our own generation by the appearance of unusual and famous puppets of diverse style. Possibly the best known is Charlie McCarthy, the "knee" puppet, developed by Edgar Bergen who, as a ventriloquist, made the dummy puppet appear to speak for himself. There are Kukla and Ollie, the sleeve puppets who performed with "Fran" in the early days of TV to bring everyday lessons to youngsters. The recent extremely popular and marvelously imaginative "Muppets" created by Jim Henson are used extensively in television for entertainment and education. The Muppets are certainly a product of their innovative creator but some aspects of their physical development must be attributed to new materials that were not available to puppeteers of previous generations. Foamed plastics and new moldable synthetic rubber can be manipulated to appear almost more lifelike than real people by the talented and nimble fingers of the puppeteers. Perhaps the Muppets, more than any other characters, have inspired classes in puppet making and performing at high schools and colleges throughout the country.

In our innovative world there is always room for something new and creative with different concepts. That is the situation with macramé puppets and gnomes. Puppets made with the simple knotting techniques of macramé are easy to create, a challenge for knotters, and a delight to use for individualized puppet performances. They can be versatile; the bodies can be quickly interchanged with an assortment of heads. They can be easily manipulated on strings as hand puppets or as knee puppets if they are perched on one's knees. They are practical and not easily damaged, given a reasonable amount of care. They can look incredibly real, depending on the size they are made. They can be stuffed or made over an armature so they are self-supporting.

The combination of puppets and gnomes is a salute to the popularity of the imaginative gnomes featured in contemporary literature. Gnomes can be given characteristics that will enable them to portray any event or lesson; any human or animal figure, or a combination of both. They are beyond reality, yet they can represent real emotions, foibles, and fears depending upon the situation.

Staging for macramé puppets and gnomes can be your own living room or stages developed specifically for the characters and the parts they are to portray. When the puppets and gnomes are not on stage, they can be equally at home perched on a couch or bed or in a corner of a room where they can observe the passing scene while preparing themselves for their next role.

The same figures developed as movable puppets may also be made as sheer decoration or as sculptural forms. However you use the patterns given, you will be introduced to macramé as a three-dimensional form that may eventually lead you to create figures and objects using your own imagination.

Materials for making macramé puppets are readily available wherever craft supplies are sold.

2. Materials for Macramé Puppets

The essential materials for macramé puppets and gnomes are any of the wide variety of macramé cord, weaving yarns, and rug yarns. With scores of distributors marketing a seemingly incredible assortment of sizes, colors, textures, and combinations of materials, it may seem formidable to select a material that is "just right" for the project you wish to make. Given the directions in the individual projects that follow, you may discover that a certain cord results in a figure twice as large as the measurements.

There is hope, of course. Nothing in macramé is ever really "wrong." If instructions indicate that a 22-inch puppet will result, you can avoid working up to a 36- or 48-inch-size figure if you will carefully observe the "mm" or "millimeter" of each cord given in the suggested materials listing. The millimeter is one of the units of measurement that the fiber industry uses to designate the diameter of a cord. Each package is marked with the "mm" that will correspond in diameter to the size of the cord in the chart illustration (page 11). Simply snip off a sample of a cord and lay it against the chart. A cord of the same diameter purchased from any distributor should yield approximately the same size figure as the one in the project.

The other variable is how tightly you knot. Generally, thick cords of about 3mm, and larger, knot up about the same for most people. Very thin cords will be knotted tightly or loosely by different knotters but heavy thicker cords cannot usually be pulled too tightly. Puppet figures should be flexible, so keep in mind that the knotting should not be so stiff and tight that the figures will not move.

Generally cords of the same "mm" thickness may be substituted for any shown in the projects. The only caution is to be careful about using very soft knotting or weaving wools and synthetics when harder textured cords such as cotton seine twine or jute are suggested. The softer cords will pull and stretch and tend to lose their shape easily. One hundred percent nylon and rayon cords are often too slippery to hold a knot and may fray while working. They should be used judiciously; they are more often suggested for adding a shiny texture to a detail (for lips or buttons) than for a complete puppet.

In addition to the basic knotting cords, a few decorating and structural materials are required and these are recommended with the project to which they apply. They include forms, such as cardboard cones and tubes, over which to shape the three-dimensional macramé. These forms are usually packaged within the spools of fibers. Other forms may be made of foamed plastic, built-up corrugated cardboard, wood, or whatever you have available that will serve the purpose.

Craft fur may be used for hair, beards, and moustaches and in some places for clothing and clothing embellishments. Some puppets require minimal stuffing in heads and bodies. The best and softist is any of the Dacron or cotton stuffing materials used for quilting and furniture fill. Old nylons are a good substitute but tend to be heavier than the cotton stuffing and may off-balance the head or body of a string puppet. You be the judge.

You will also need scrap pieces of leather and suede fabrics for clothing if a particular project suggests clothes. Often the clothing is the macramé knotting itself. Buttons, beads, and buckles are also suggested in specific projects.

For decorating the puppets, waterproof felt-tip markers, acrylic paints, and brushes are required. Entire heads or details can be made with the papier-mâché and cloth-draping method described on pages 87–89.

You will also need the control devices for a particular puppet. String puppets require a transparent manipulating string, made of fishline or other heavy nylon string, and a wood control bar. Hand puppets require that you camouflage your thumb and forefinger with a glove that can be made from a felt panel or by using a real glove. For larger puppets, you may wish to make an entire sleeve so that your arm does not poke up above the stage level and dispel the illusion you are trying to create.

Rulers, scissors, and T pins are essential to macramé. Additional materials required for specific figures are listed with the projects.

NOTE: Instructions and materials are presented in good faith, but no warranty is given nor results guaranteed by the author or the publisher.

Control or manipulating bars for the puppet strings can be made from any thin wood scraps with nylon fishline as the working cords. A glove can be used to camouflage your hand inside a hand puppet.

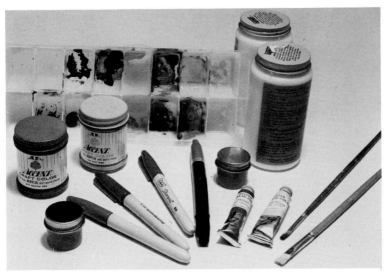

Decorate puppet heads and other details by brushing on with acrylic paints; felt-tip markers are also useful and convenient.

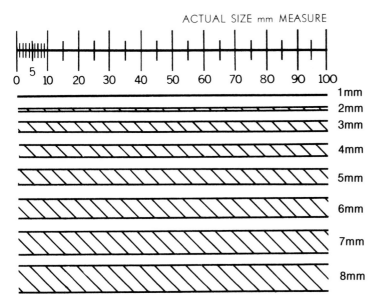

ACTUAL SIZE mm MEASURE

0 5 10 20 30 40 50 60 70 80 90 100

1mm
2mm
3mm
4mm
5mm
6mm
7mm
8mm

ACTUAL CORD THICKNESSES

CORD SIZE CHART
Actual thickness of a cord can be determined by placing it against the chart. When you know the thickness in mm, any brand cord may be used that fits the size chart to yield the size puppet called for in the pattern.

3. Your Knotting Vocabulary

The two basic macramé knots are the Square Knot and the Clove Hitch. Other auxiliary knots are used for mounting the cords, for endings, and for other decorative and functional purposes. Variations of the basic knots used in the projects are illustrated. The following knots apply to all and some of the individual projects. Where specific knotting procedures apply to one project, they are shown with the project's development. (NOTE: The same knots may be referred to by different names in many books.) A "sennit" is a length of knotted cord.

Mounting Knot—Lark's Head

The Lark's Head is an auxiliary knot used for mounting one cord to another, or to a bar or ring. It may be used for a project's beginning and for increasing within the knotted fabric.

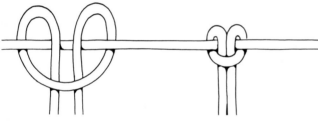

Bend a length of cord in half. Place the bend *over* and about an inch above the holding cord. Fold the bend of the working cord down and behind the holding cord. Pull the ends of the working cord through the bend from front to back.

Pull the ends to tighten.

Reverse Lark's Head results when the folded cord is placed *under* the holding cord with the bend at the top. The bend is folded down and the loose ends are pulled through from the back to the front.

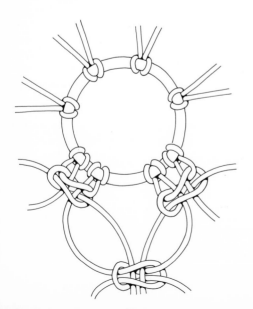

← The Lark's Head may be mounted on a ring, then the working cords developed into square knotting.

→ The Lark's Head can be tied over a series of anchor cords in chainlike sennits.

The Square Knot

The Square Knot, one of the basic macramé knots, is incredibly versatile. In its simplest construction it is tied with four elements (or strands) using the two outer elements for knotting, the two inside elements for anchors. Often, many elements are combined for anchors or for knotting to increase the diameter of an area, to change patterns and multiples of working cords, to increase and decrease a shape.

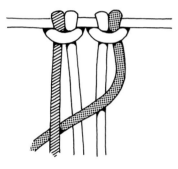

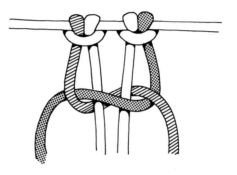

A. Bring the right cord *over* and to the left of the two center cords (anchors) and place the left cord *over* the right.

B. Bring the left cord *under* the right, *behind* both anchors and *through* the loop formed by the right cord and then *over* the right cord.

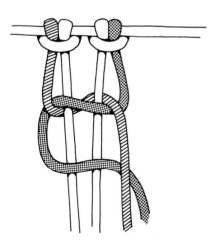

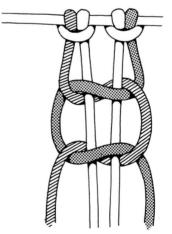

C. Repeat same procedure from the other side: Place the left cord *over* the anchors and the right cord *over* the left.

D. Place the right *under* the left *behind* the anchors and *through* the loop formed by the left cord and *over* the left cord. Pull each half of the knot tight to result in the completed Square Knot.

The Alternating Square Knot

Combining the right half of one group of cords with the left half of the adjacent group to form a new set of cords results in the Alternating Square Knot pattern shown.

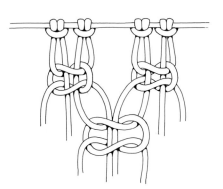

Different numbers of cords used in alternating progressions and in solidly and loosely tied areas and in designs that move from one side to another provide the variations required in the patterns.

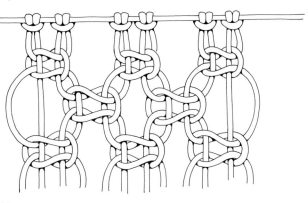

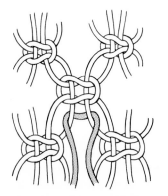
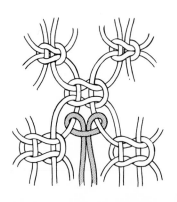

To increase Square Knotting cords in Alternating Square Knotting fabric, link new cords around anchor cords as shown in top two drawings and pick them up for knotting in the next row as necessary. *To decrease,* drop cords behind the fabric, cut off, and tuck ends into the knotting so they are unobtrusive. A crochet hook is handy for pulling loose ends through.

Square Knot Mounting

The Half Knot and Half Knot Twist

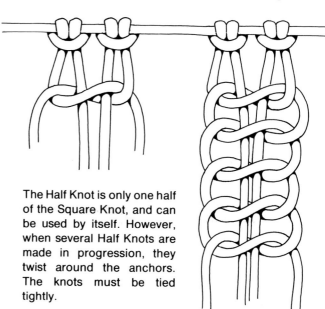

The Square Knot may be used for mounting cords directly onto a ring. Fold two cords and bend over the ring to yield four working ends. Use two cords for knotting and two for anchors.

The Half Knot is only one half of the Square Knot, and can be used by itself. However, when several Half Knots are made in progression, they twist around the anchors. The knots must be tied tightly.

A succession of Half Knot Twists, *right*.

Reverse Square Knot

Left

By exchanging the anchor cords of the Square Knot with the working cords for one knot sequence, a "joint" can be achieved. This is used in the elbows and knees of the Gnome puppets.

The Square Knot Button

Below

The button is made by tying three or more Square Knots and pulling them up into a loop by inserting the anchors over the first Square Knot. All the cords move up to form the button and the knotting cords are brought down from the back and continue to be used for another button or for a continuation of Square Knot sennits.

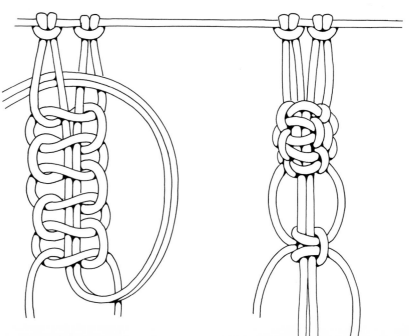

The Clove Hitch

The Clove Hitch (also called the Double Half Hitch) is a looped macramé knot with several variations. The knotting cord is looped twice
over an anchor cord, rod or ring. It may be tied in horizontal, vertical,
and diagonal directions. It can be tied from right to left and from left
to right. The direction of the anchor determines the direction of the
knotted pattern.

Horizontal Clove Hitch

Hold the anchor taut *over* the
knotting cords. Each knotting cord is looped twice
around the anchor and tight-
ened to appear as shown in
the finished knots.

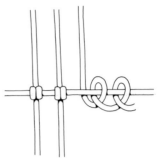

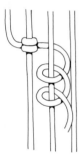

Diagonal Clove Hitch

For a diagonal or oblique
line, hold the anchor at the
angle you require and tie the
working cords in the Clove
Hitch.

Vertical Clove Hitch

The same knot worked ver-
tically uses one length of
cord for tying all the knots;
*each strand of knotting cord
changes its role* and be-
comes an anchor as the
knotting cord is tied over it.

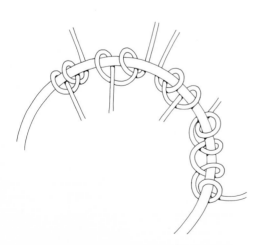

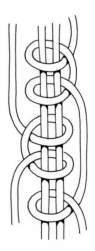

Mounting with a Clove Hitch

A Clove Hitch can be used for
mounting or for adding a ring
in the body of an object.

Clove Hitch Chains

Variations can be made with
a combination of Clove
Hitches tied from left to right
then from right to left over
several holding cords.

Half Hitch

Only one loop of the Clove Hitch results in the Half Hitch. Knots may be made over one or over multiple anchor cords.

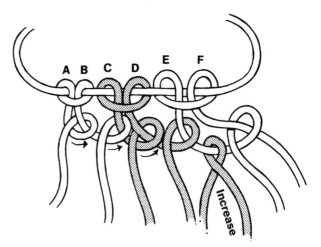

Spiral Half Hitch

A spiraling effect is achieved by working a Half Hitch over an adjacent cord and around a shape rather than the usual method of working the knots over separate anchor cords. In essence, each cord becomes the anchor for the cord next to it. A shape may be easily increased by introducing a new folded cord into the work.

Spiral Clove Hitch

The same effect can be achieved with a Clove Hitch worked onto the adjacent cord to achieve a webbing or a tighter spiraled knotting fabric.

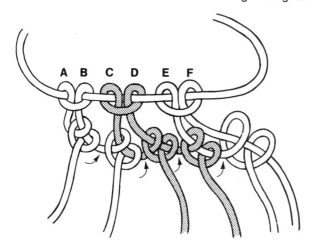

Wrapping

Wrapping several cords together is essential for endings and for grouping cords within sennits. Sometimes you will wrap with one of the knotting cords as shown in the first wrapping method (left). Or you may introduce an added cord of another or the same color.

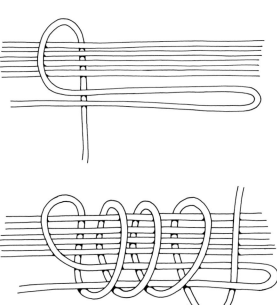

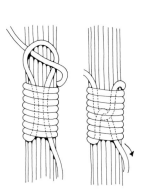

To wrap cords using one of the lengths in the sennit, form a loop with one end of the cord and hold the bottom of the group of cords secure. Wrap the cord around all and place the end through the loop. Pull down on the loop pulling the end inside. Clip off any loose ends.

Introduce a new length of cord parallel to the lengths you want to gather in the wrap. Lay out as shown, above. Below, wrap the cord around all the strands and pull the strand (A) which will bring the loop and the loose end under the wraps. The wrapping should be done very tightly (it is drawn loosely for demonstration).

To Simplify Working . . . Use the Butterfly

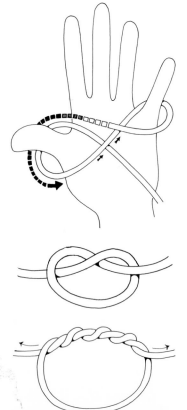

When there are many lengths of long cords to be worked and they tend to tangle, wrap one or more cords into the Butterfly. Wind the cord, as shown, and secure with a rubberband around the bundle. The working cord will slip out of the bundle as you pull it gently.

The Overhand Knot

The Overhand Knot is used to tie at cord ends to prevent fraying. It can be used to secure square knots and hitches. It can be tied with one or multiple cords or various arrangements.

When several Overhand Knots are placed within a loop, the ends are pulled to result . . .

. . . in the Coil Knot, which is decorative and useful for ends and for keeping beads on strands.

Tassels

Tassels are used extensively for finishing.

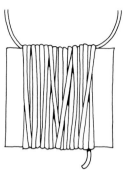

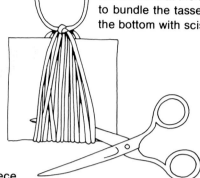

Tie the cord at the top tightly to bundle the tassel and cut the bottom with scissors.

Wrap cords around a piece of stiff cardboard the length you want the tassel to be. Place a tie cord at the top under the wrap.

Wrap another length of cord down about one inch or more (depending upon the tassel length) and tie tightly.

Unraveled plies can be an attractive ending for unknotted lengths of cords and for tassels. Simply unwind the plies and fluff them out. You can use a wire brush or a comb for additional texturing.

Braiding may be used for detailing a puppet's clothing or for pigtails of hairdos. Basic braids are made with three elements worked in this sequence:

2 over 1; 3 over 2; 1 over 3.

4. Projects

Designer, Pattie Frazer

PROJECT 1

BOZO, THE STRING PUPPET CLOWN

String puppets are designed to be loose and flexible so all their joints move easily and fluidly. They are manipulated by crossbars held above stage-top level; the strings attached to the crossbars hold the major portions of the body—the head, knees, arms. As you become proficient with the manipulations, more strings may be attached so that elbows and wrists can be controlled, and/or ankles and knees, for greater expressiveness.

The same kind of body may be used to develop other characters by changing color schemes, heads, facial characteristics, and hats. Try the clown body with a gnome head; dress it in different kinds of clothing.

Bodies may also be made so the heads are interchangeable by simply untying the knot that is used through the head in Construction Step H.

Materials

All Patterns Actual Size

16 yards white rug yarn (for body), approximately 4mm (see cord size chart, p. 11)

18 yards red rug yarn (for hair and pompons), approximately 4mm

11 yards red braided nylon macramé cord (for body) 3 to 3.5mm

5 yards 10-lb. test fishline (for puppet string controls)

1 head approximately 4″ high and 3½″ in diameter, hollow on inside. Use a part of a gourd, OR a foamed plastic ball with center hollowed, OR papier-mâché over foamed plastic, OR a ready-made head from a craft shop with a hole in the center top.

Parts of the gourd, OR wood, OR foam board for

Hands   2 pieces 3″ x 3½″

Shoes   2 pieces 5″ x 2¾″

Use a drill to make holes in hands and shoes as shown in pattern.

Three lengths of wood, each approximately 10″ x 1″ x ⅜″ for the control bar

1 wood dowel ¼″ in diameter and 4¾″ long for shoulder bar

5 screw eyes 4¾″ long

4 tacks ⅝″ long to tack the wood control bars (Fig. 1-D, pages 26–27)

White glue

White acrylic paint and paintbrushes

Red acrylic paint or nail polish

Black narrow felt-tip pen

Finished Size

Overall Length of Puppet, 25".
Macramé Portion, Neck to Feet, 21".
Length of Each Arm, 11".

Instructions

1. PREPARE HEAD, SHOES, AND HANDS

   Head: Use patterns, pages 24–26.

Step A. Prepare head from gourd or foamed plastic with cardboard collar. Paint white with red features (Fig. 1-C).

Step B. Cut hands and shoes from patterns (Figs. 1-B and 1-E). Paint tops and bottoms white. Add red on the fingers and shoes' detailing.

Step C. Paint with white the ends and tips of the dowel to be used for the shoulder bar.

2. KNOTTING

   Body and Arms:

   CUT

White Rug Yarn:	4 lengths, 8 feet each, for body
	4 lengths, 4 feet each, for arms
Red Braided Cord:	4 lengths, 5 feet each, for body
	4 lengths, 3 feet each, for arms

Step A. Double the cords, and mount onto the dowel rod with Lark's Head as follows:

LEFT ARM	BODY	RIGHT ARM
1 white arm cord	1 white body cord	1 white arm cord
2 red arm cords	2 red body cords	2 red arm cords
1 white arm cord	2 white body cords	1 white arm cord
	2 red body cords	
	1 white body cord	

Step B. Square knot each group of four cords as separate lengths. Each group will consist of two white working cords for knotting with the red cords in the center.

Step C. Knot the left arm for 11 inches.

Step D. Knot the two sets of body cords 21 inches.

Step E. Knot the right arm cords for 11 inches. Allow the red cords to hang long. Secure the white ends by knotting and working loose ends back up into knots. Cut off, and dab glue on ends if necessary.

Step F. Tie the shoes onto the legs. Insert the red cords down through Hole 1 and up through Hole 2 and tie in bows as for shoelaces.

Step G. Tie the hands onto the red cords of the arms by inserting cords down through holes and securing with a knot. Trim off. Glue to secure if necessary.

Step H. Tie a 15-inch length of yarn around dowel below neck, and bring up through center of head to hole in top. Tie in a knot, but do not cut off: the ends will be used to tie on the yarn wig (Fig. 1-A).

Step I. Make two tassels and hair (page 19). Cut a piece of cardboard 1½ inches wide by 5 inches long. For each 3-inch tassel:
Wrap 2 yards red yarn around the 1½-inch width of the cardboard 25 times. Tie all the cords securely at one end and cut the other end. Fluff out. Use the tied ends to tie one tassel at clown's neck just under the dowel rod and over the two central white cords. Tie the other tassel across the center white cords at the fifth knot below the dowel to hold the lengths together and form the body.

Step J. For the hair: Wrap 14 yards red yarn around the 8-inch length of the cardboard about 50 times (100 ends). Tie around one end, and cut off. Spread out, and cut bangs by trimming about 20 of the lengths short. Spread the yarn and shape so the yarns are longer in back to simulate a wig. Tie the yarn wig onto the head with white cord protruding through head hole. Knot and clip off.

3. ASSEMBLING

Assemble the puppet strings and control bars:

Step A. Nail the bars together as shown (Fig. 1-D). Allow about 3 inches at the end of Bar 1 to hold the control. Place a screw eye ½ inch from the end. Place a screw eye about ½ inch from each end of each crossbar (2 and 3).

Step B. Puppet Strings. Cut the fishline into 5 one-yard lengths. Secure as follows:
Tie one length from the top of the head, securing it under the yarn knot, to the screw eye on Bar 1.
Tie one length from the top of each wrist, securing it to the yarn knots and to each screw eye on Bar 2.
Tie one length from each knee to each screw eye on Bar 3.
NOTE: The screw eyes will all protrude from the *bottom* of the bars facing the puppet.

Step C. Work the puppet and adjust the lengths of control strings as necessary. The head string will be the shortest, the arm strings longer; the knee strings will be longest.

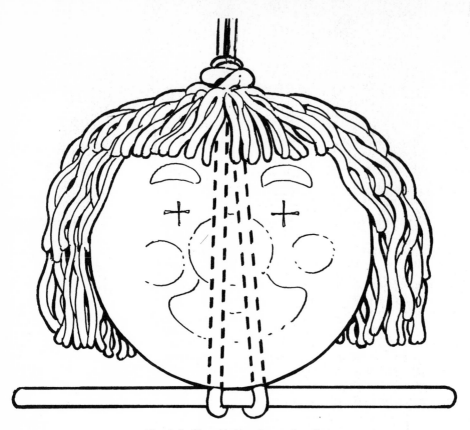

Fig. 1-A. Step H. Head construction

left shoe

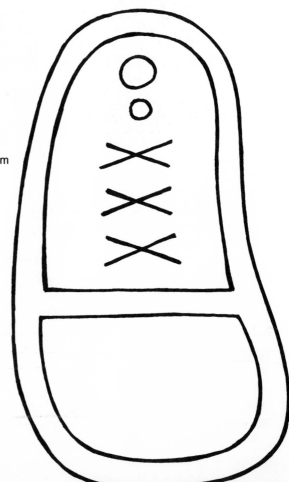

Fig. 1-B. Shoe patterns' actual size. Cut from gourd pieces, thin wood, or foam board.

MR. GNOME

BINGO, String Puppet

WOODLAND GNOMES: Boy and Girl

PETEY, THE PEACOCK

WACKY WILLIE

MRS. GNOME

BOZO, Red-and-White Clown
String Puppet

Indian Maiden Hand Puppet

Clowning Around

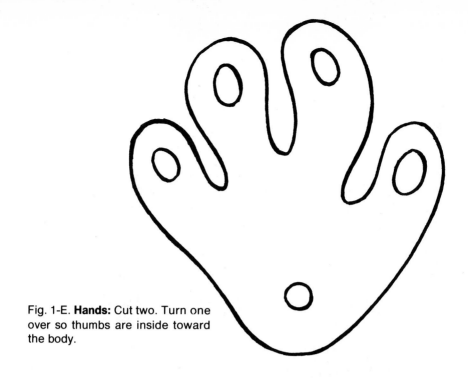

Fig. 1-E. **Hands:** Cut two. Turn one over so thumbs are inside toward the body.

right shoe

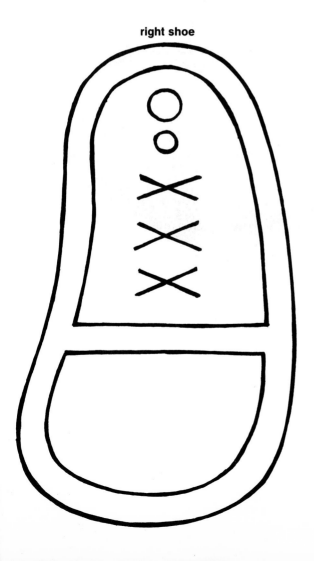

Fig. 1-C. **Face:** Actual size. Features are red with black outlines on white background.

Fig. 1-D. **Control Bar:** Size shown may be approximated if actual sizes of wood are not available.

3

2

○ —Screw eyes to attach strings

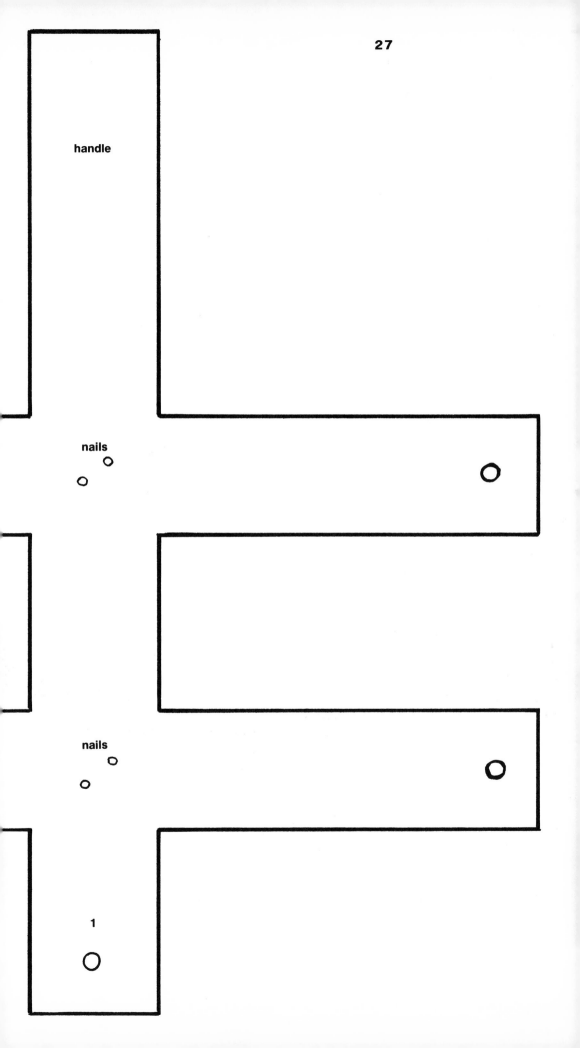

Designer, Pattie Frazer

PROJECT 2

BINGO—A STRING PUPPET

If the knot used in this tubular puppet is new to you, it is because its introduction to macramé is probably new here. But it is the basic Half Hitch tied to form a tubular shape. When two colors are used, a spiraling design appears. The knot is delightfully adaptable to puppet bodies because it gives dimension, and the right amount of solidity when soft or firm cords are used, yet it is supple enough to be manipulated by puppet strings. The body, in a tube form, becomes more believable as a figure than with flat knotting.

Pattie Frazer developed this whimsical puppet using the Spiral Half Hitch in blue and white synthetic rug yarn. The yarn is thick and the knotting works up so quickly that you will have the body shape completed in a couple of hours. The head shown is cut from a portion of a gourd; the hands and shoes are also cut from the remaining gourd parts. But you can make the same shaping with a foamed plastic ball for a head and a cone of cardboard for a collar (directions are given on page 86).

Use this same Spiral Half Hitch to make a family of string puppets with any facial and clothing characteristics you like. Shapes may be made short and squat by adding cords; they may be thinned by decreasing and dropping ends inside the knotting.

Materials

12 yards white rug yarn, approximately 4mm

12 yards blue rug yarn, approximately 4mm

1 piece lightweight plywood approximately 6" x 10" x ¼" thick for hands and feet. Cut out using patterns pages 32 and 35.

1 gourd approximately 4½" in diameter OR a foamed plastic ball 4" in diameter for head with a circle of manila cardboard 5½" in diameter for neck

1 dowel 4" long and ¼" in diameter (or a stick) to be used for shoulder bar

2 Plastic Craft eyes ⅝" in diameter

White acrylic paint and paintbrush

Black acrylic paint or permanent felt-tip marker

Blue acrylic paint or permanent felt-tip marker

5" x 3" piece of green Craft Fur for hair

5" x 3" piece of blue Craft Fur for hair

3 pieces wood approximately 10" x 1" x ⅜" for the control bar (see pattern pages 26–27)

4 tacks ⅝" long to tack wood control bars together

5 small screw eyes ⅝" long

White glue

Approximately 5 yards 10-pound-test clear nylon fishing line

Finished Size

Puppet Overall 26½".
Length of Macramé 22".
Arms, each 10½" long.

Instructions

1.   PREPARE HEAD, SHOES, AND HANDS

Step A.   *Make the head* approximately 4½" high and 4" in diameter and 5½" diameter around neck, cut from a gourd, or use a 4" foamed plastic ball. Drill a hole in center of head from neck to top. If foamed plastic is used add a collar made of cardboard, using the pattern given in Fig. 2-J. Cover collar and foam with draped fabric or papier-mâché (pages 86–89).

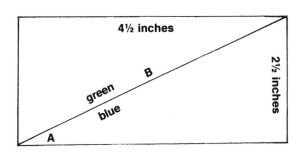

Fig. 2-B. Hair piece. Cut one triangle of each color to sizes shown. Move triangles so A of the blue meets B on the green. Glue to head.

Step B.   *For the hair,* glue on 2 pieces of Craft Fur using ½ green, ½ blue. Plan a 2½" x 4½" rectangle of the 2 colors, as in Fig. 2-B, and cut in triangles. Separate the 2 triangles and glue to head so point A of the blue is about halfway along the green at point B and the fur covers the head as shown in the photo.

Step C.   *Make the shoes and hands* from pieces of the gourd or use wood about ⅜" thick. Cut from patterns, pages 32–33. Drill holes. Paint pieces white on top and bottom. Add black trim, as shown, with paint or waterproof felt-tip marker.

2.   KNOTTING

Body

Cut 4 white cords each 16 feet long
Cut 4 blue cords each 16 feet long

Step A.   Double and mount 2 white, 2 blue, 2 white, 2 blue cords on the dowel rod with a Lark's Head Knot.

Step B.   Tie all cords around in the tube shape with the Spiral Half Hitch for 6 inches.

Step C.   Separate the cords for the legs using 8 lengths for each leg: 4 working lengths of white and 4 working lengths of blue. Knot for 17 inches.

Step D.   Finish at bottom by tying all cords into one knot and pushing ends up into leg at ankle.

Arms

Cut 4 white cords each 8 feet long
Cut 4 blue cords each 8 feet long

Step E.   Mount 2 white and 2 blue cords through and around the loops of the body cord knots at each side (shoulder position).

Step F.   Tie each arm in the Spiral Half Hitch for 10½ inches. Finish as for ankles.

Fig. 2-C. **SPIRAL HALF HITCH**

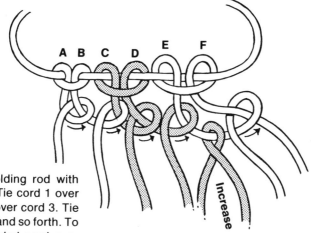

Mount cords to holding rod with Lark's Head Knot. Tie cord 1 over cord 2. Tie cord 2 over cord 3. Tie cord 3 over cord 4, and so forth. To increase, add a folded cord over one of the bars, as shown. When two or more colors are used, the colors will form a spiral design.

3. ASSEMBLING

Step A.   If head form is not hollow, make a hole through the center from neck to top of head. Attach head to dowel at shoulders with 2 lengths of 18″ cord; one at each side. Double the cord, mount on dowel with Lark's Head, and bring ends up through head to center and knot to secure at top of head. (See head construction, Step H, Bozo the Clown, page 24.)

Step B. Tie shoes to each leg and hands to each arm with a short length of yarn inserted through the knotting and down through holes in hands and shoes. Knot at bottoms; glue knots to secure.

Step C. Glue shoulder dowel to underpart of collar.

Step D. Glue on plastic eyes.

Step E. To attach puppet strings assemble the control pieces of wood by nailing together as shown on pages 26–27 as for the Bozo.

Step F. Place screw eyes at positions shown. Cut nylon fish-line into 5 lengths and tie nylon line to Board 1 screw eye and at top of puppet head. Tie one line from each wrist to screw eyes on Board 2. Tie one line from each knee to screw eyes on Board 3.

Step G. Adjust the lengths of the puppet strings so you can handle the puppet and make it perform. The line to the head will be the shortest, the lines to the arms longer, and the lines to the knees the longest. The screw eyes will face downward toward the puppet.

Fig. 2-D. **Shoes**

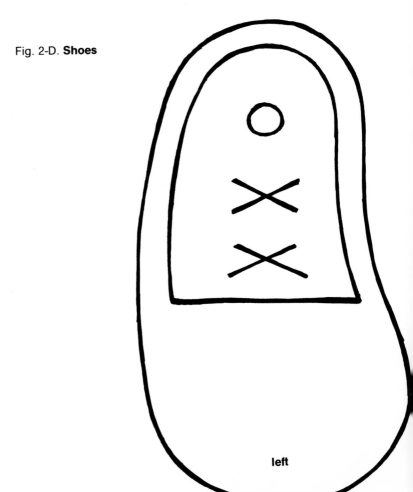

left

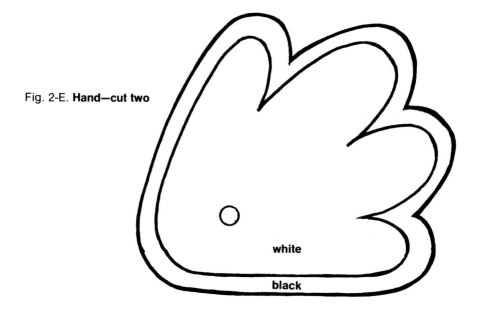

Fig. 2-E. **Hand—cut two**

white

black

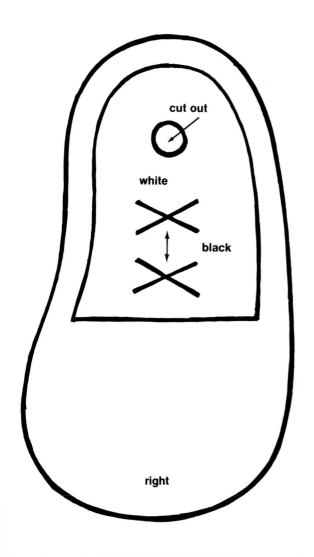

cut out

white

black

right

black

Fig. 2-F. Face pattern—actual size
Glue on craft eyes or draw in.

← black

blue

Fig. 2-G-H. Other face designs optional for additional characters

top

fold

cut

Fig. 2-I. **Neck tube**
Roll side to side and insert through Hole A in collar. Cut on dotted lines and glue cut tabs inside collar to form neck tube.

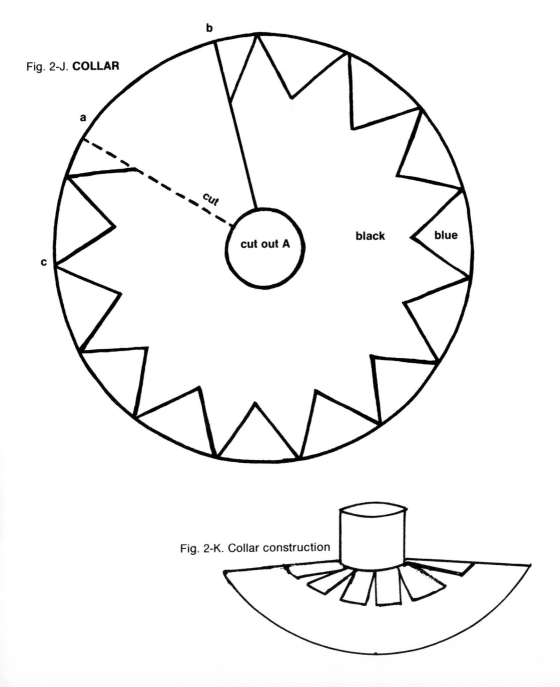

Fig. 2-J. **COLLAR**

b

a

cut

cut out A

black   blue

c

Fig. 2-K. Collar construction

Designer, Dona Meilach

WACKY WILLIE

Wacky Willie is so wonderful to work, you'll want to make a whole family for him after you realize how simple he is to create. With your materials gathered and your cords all cut, you can tie a Wacky Willie in a couple of hours. Use the Spiral Half Hitch (page 17) for covering the foamed plastic balls, then tie on as many cords as you like for a fluffy mane.

Materials

14 yards white cotton cable cord, 3mm
19 yards kelly green jute, 3mm
 6 yards black rug yarn or knitting yarn
 2 yards ribbon 1'' wide in 2 different col.ors
One cardboard tube about 8'' long, ¾'' in diameter
Three 3''-diameter foamed plastic balls
 1 knife or hot wire to cut one ball
 2 craft eyes ⅝'' in diameter
 1 sheet black construction paper
 1 pencil
 1 wide-pointed black felt-tip marker
 2 pieces of wood each 10½'' x 1¼'' x ⅜'' for control
 4 screw eyes ⅝'' long
 2 tacks ⅝'' long
 4 yards nylon fishline

Finished Size

Approximately 18 inches long from tip of nose to end of body, plus tail.

Instructions

1. KNOTTING

    Cut the following cords:

For the head and neck cut	For the tail cut
3 white cords each 3 yards long	6 white cords about 1 foot long
1 green cord 3 yards long	6 green cords about 1 foot long
For the torso cut	1 green cord 2 feet long
3 green cords each 1 yard long	For the mane cut
For the legs cut	24 green cords each 8 inches long
2 green cords each 7 feet long	12 black cords each 8 inches long
2 white cords each 4 feet long	

Head, Neck and Body:
Fold in half and mount 3 white 3-yard cords with Lark's Heads onto the center of the 3-yard green cord. Pin these central knots around the hole of a ¾'' diameter cardboard tube. Tie the green cord around the tube top and use these green cord ends for knotting along with the white cords.

37

Rows 1–6   Tie the cords in Spiral Half Hitches around tube to make nose. Remove tube.

Rows 7–8   Shape one foamed plastic ball into an oval head by compressing 2 opposite sides lightly against a flat table top. Pin the knotting to the front of the oval head with the loose cords extending over the flattened ball; the flat sides will be cheeks. Knot around the ball for 2 rows. The knots will be spaced farther apart on the head than those in the nose.

Row 9   Increase with a green 1-yard cord folded over a loop in the previous row next to an existing free cord. Knot all around.

Rows 10–16
(Approx.)   Shape knotting around head and work the cord ends to the lower back portion of the head.

Rows 17–34   Neck. Allow ends of added 1-yard cord to protrude at top back of head. Push cardboard tube up against foamed plastic egg at neck and continue knotting with original 3 white and 1 green cord for 17 rows, or 7½ inches, over tube. Remove tube.

Torso and Legs

Prepare the foamed plastic ball for the torso as for the head, lightly compressing two sides. Make a hole through the foamed plastic with a pencil about ⅓ of the way from the back for the legs (as shown in Fig. 3-B). Make the legs by threading two green 7-foot cords and two white 4-foot cords through the hole. Center the cords in the hole and tie Square Knot sennits on each side of the ball knotting with the green over the white filler cords. Secure ends temporarily with an Overhand Knot or rubberband.

Row 35   *Torso Knotting:* Pin the neck end to the foamed plastic ball and tie Spiral Half Hitches.

Row 36   Increase with two folded 1-yard green cords around loops in the previous row, placing one at each side of the back. Tie all around.

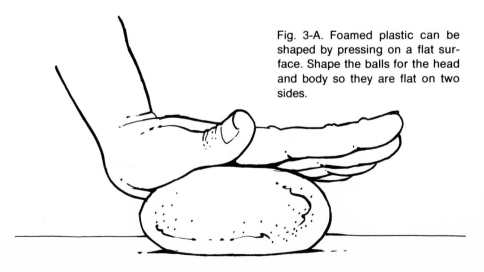

Fig. 3-A. Foamed plastic can be shaped by pressing on a flat surface. Shape the balls for the head and body so they are flat on two sides.

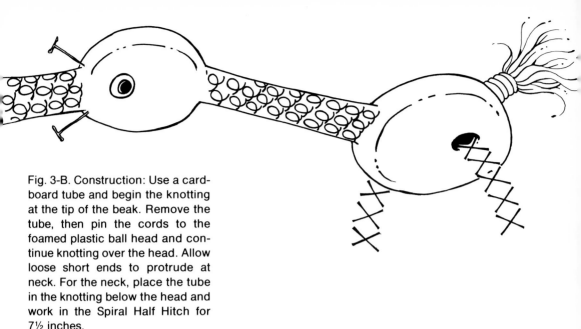

Fig. 3-B. Construction: Use a cardboard tube and begin the knotting at the tip of the beak. Remove the tube, then pin the cords to the foamed plastic ball head and continue knotting over the head. Allow loose short ends to protrude at neck. For the neck, place the tube in the knotting below the head and work in the Spiral Half Hitch for 7½ inches.

Rows 37–42   Continue shaping knots all around foamed plastic torso ball and allowing legs to extend through knotting in the proper position.

2. FINISHING

Tail

Fold the 1-foot lengths of white and green along the knotting cord ends. Wrap all together with the 2-foot length of green for about 1". Trim ends evenly and unply for fluffy tail.

Mane and Neck

Add the 8" lengths of green and black along top of head over the knotting cords with Lark's Heads. Trim evenly and unply ends. Optional: Cut additional cords and add around neck if you like. Tie ribbons in a big beautiful bow around the neck.

Eyes and Lashes

Glue on eyes. Make eyelashes from black construction paper (Figs. 3-D and E). For each lash, roll a piece of 1½" x 3" paper around a pencil. Secure with tape or rubber-band for several hours. Remove from pencil and cut to shape. Fringe on one side with the scissors. Pin or glue on head above eye. If you pin the lash to the foamed plastic it can be changed easily to make the eye appear closed or open, or if the paper becomes messy.

Feet

Cut one foamed plastic ball in half. (See Fig. 3-C, page 40.) Flatten the rounded top slightly. Make a hole through the center with a pencil. Impress a slightly larger area around the hole on the flat, or bottom, of the foot. Untie the holding knot from each foot. Thread the 4 cords through the foot from top to bottom on each side and tie white cords with green in Overhand Knots to secure. Trim ends and "Countersink" the knots in the impressed portion around the hole. Draw details on feet to simulate hoofs with the wide-pointed felt-tip marker.

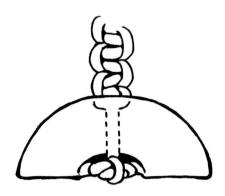

Fig. 3-C. Foot construction: Cut one foamed plastic ball in half. With a pencil, make a hole through it from the curve to the flat side. String the cords down through the hole. Make an impression in the bottom of the foot with the end of the pencil. Knot the cords and push the knot up into the impression.

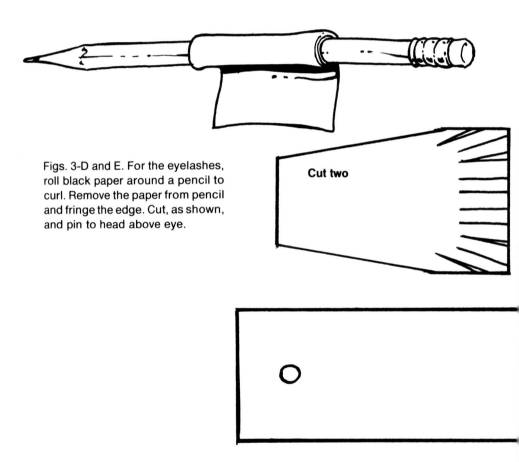

Figs. 3-D and E. For the eyelashes, roll black paper around a pencil to curl. Remove the paper from pencil and fringe the edge. Cut, as shown, and pin to head above eye.

Cut two

3.   ASSEMBLING

Attach puppet control cords and manipulating boards. Cut 2 wood control bars (Fig. 3-F) and tie on nylon strings as shown in Fig. 3-G: one to the center of the head, one to the center top of the body, one to each knee.

Figs. 3-F and G. Control bar. Attach cords as shown.

Designer, Bob West

PROJECT 4

GNOMES

Gnomes, the subjects of entire books and millions of imaginations, can be inspired additions to your family. Make them for decoration and use them as conversation pieces. They look marvelous perched on a couch or lounging on a bed or other piece of furniture. They're whimsical, wonderful.

Make them, too, as stuffed dolls for your youngsters. With strings attached, they can become puppets willing to bend to your every script change. They are large enough to be propped on the knee and worked in the style of the ventriloquist carrying on conversations with his creator and his audience.

Designer Bob West made the gnomes from white cotton seine twine. The macramé bodies are stuffed with Dacron inserted into a nylon stocking. The stuffed nylon is also the basis for the face.

Soft sculpture faces can be so expressive; they are easy to make with a little practice. You pinch up the features and stitch them into place with needle and thread—you'll feel like a plastic surgeon, shaping and manipulating the features. Make them imaginative or try to make them look like someone you know, then give them for gifts to the person they're representing.

The creation of gnomes, whether figments of your imagination or takeoffs on real people, is one of the newest applications of macramé. The male and female gnomes are made essentially the same, but with alterations in the shaping of the body, the features, and the clothing. Only the basic knots are used: The entire body is made with Alternating Square Knots and some wrapping. The instructions may appear lengthy, but after you tackle the project, it is quite simple to develop.

MR. GNOME

Materials
180 yards (540 feet) #72 white cotton seine twine
20 yards (60 feet) #18 white cotton seine twine
  1 light-colored nylon stocking
  1 package Dacron batting
  1 piece of red-brown Craft Fur 4" x 10" for hair and beard
  1 piece of brown suede, approx. 18" x 27"
  1 bell
  2 black wooden beads ½" in diameter for eyes
  1 buckle 2" high and 1¼" wide
White heavy cotton sewing thread
  2 yards brown waxed linen for sewing hat
  1 long feather
One ¼" wood dowel 12" long

Tools

Leather sewing needle	T pins
Leather or paper punch	Scissors

Finished Size

Top of cap to toes: approximately 41 inches.

Instructions

1. KNOTTING

Step A. *Body*

Cut 20 cords of #72 twine, each 20 feet long. Place 12 T pins on a macramé board about ¼″ apart. Fold 12 cords in half, and place one cord on each T pin at the fold (do not use a Lark's Head). This begins the upper torso at the neckline.

Square Knot: Use 4 working ends per knot to yield 6 sets of Square Knotted cords. Follow the body knotting chart and work completely in alternating Square Knots. Tie the knots tightly.

BODY KNOTTING CHART

Key:
- X = one full Square Knot (4 working ends)
- ‖ = two unused cords
- **X** = add one double cord (2 ends)
- ⊗ = one full Square Knot added (4 working ends)

Row	Knotting pattern	Number of knots
1	X X X X X X	6
2	‖ X X X X X ‖	5
3	X X X X X X	6
4	**X** X X X X X **X**	7
5	‖ X X X X X X ‖	6
6	X X X X X X X	7
7	**X** X X X X X X **X**	8
8	‖ X X X X X X X ‖	7
9	⊗ X X X X X X X X ⊗	10

Row 10   Begin to work in a circle in Alternating Square Knots.

Rows 11–20   Continue to work in a circle, making the knots looser, about ½″ apart, to shape the stomach.

Row 21   Pull the knots in this row together tightly.

Step B. *Legs*

Divide the cords in half, using 5 knots in a circle for each leg, and tie:

Rows 1–12   Alternating Square Knots for upper leg

Row 13   Reverse Square Knots for knee joints

Rows 14–29   Alternating Square Knots for lower leg

Step C.   *Feet*

For each foot: Separate cords into knotting groups as follows and work toward body front (the front is where the body is open in Rows 1 to 10). Follow foot knotting chart.

SEPARATE GROUPS: 4 cords   12 cords   4 cords

Row 1   Use the 4 cords at each side to tie one large Square Knot over the 12 center cords.

SEPARATE GROUPS: 8 cords   4 cords   8 cords

Row 2   Tie one Square Knot at each side, using 8 cords in each. Knot over the 4 center cords.

Rows 3–4   Tie 3 Square Knots with cords divided so
Rows 3–4   Tie 3 Square Knots with cords divided so there are 4 cords in the center and 8 cords in each end group.

Row 5   Begin top of foot with Alternating Square Knots. Counting from left: Tie 2 Square Knots with cords 4 to 8 and 13 to 16 (use 2 center cords for each). The untied end cords will be used to knot the top of foot or shoe.

Rows 6–16

NOTE: Drop 2 end cords from *each row;* these end cords will be used to form shoe top. The sole portion will become narrower.

Row 6   5 Alternating Square Knots (be sure to drop 2 end cords and in all following rows)

Row 7   4 Alternating Square Knots

Row 8   3 Alternating Square Knots

Row 9   4 Alternating Square Knots

Row 10   3 Alternating Square Knots

Row 11   2 Alternating Square Knots

Row 12   3 Alternating Square Knots

Row 13   2 Alternating Square Knots

Row 14   1 Alternating Square Knot

Row 15   2 Alternating Square Knots

Row 16   1 Alternating Square Knot

FOOT KNOTTING CHART

Row	1	2	3	4	5	6	7	8	9	
1					X					
2			X				X			
3			X		X		X			
4			X		X		X			
5				X		X				←start top of foot
6		X		X	X	X		X		
7			X	X	X	X	X			
8				X	X	X				
9			X	X	X	X	X			
10				X	X	X				
11				X	X					
12				X	X	X				
13				X	X					
14					X					
15				X	X					
16					X					

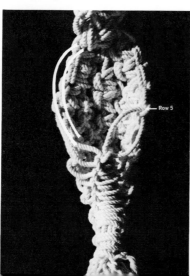

— Row 5

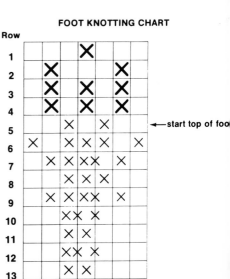

Photo 4-1. Foot detail. The end cords at the fifth row become the top portion of the foot.

Step D.   *Top of Foot*

Pick up the end cords from Row 5; use one cord on each side for knotting. All remaining cords are used as fillers within the Square Knot (see photo for construction). Continue in each row, using one each end cord for the knot with the other cords in the center. With each row, the central cords will increase, and this vertical group will become thicker and narrower to form the toe.

Photo 1. Tie last knot very tightly, and insert ends up into foot so it won't loosen. Center cords become toe ends. Unply and fluff out. Repeat the same knotting progression for the other foot, and match knot sizes so feet are the same. Use a scrap length of twine (Fig. 4-A) to knot the top of the foot to the back and give it an ankle shape. Tie one string at each side of each foot.

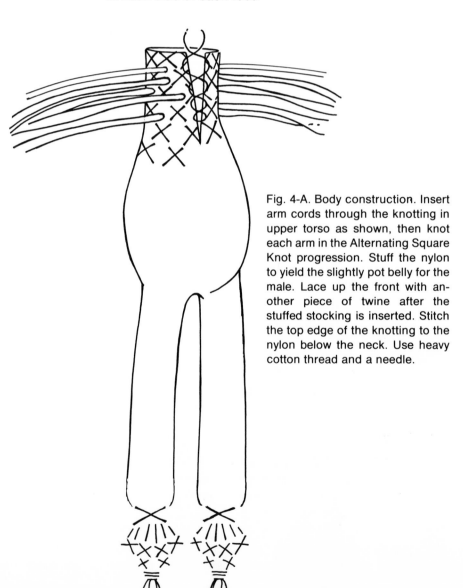

Fig. 4-A. Body construction. Insert arm cords through the knotting in upper torso as shown, then knot each arm in the Alternating Square Knot progression. Stuff the nylon to yield the slightly pot belly for the male. Lace up the front with another piece of twine after the stuffed stocking is inserted. Stitch the top edge of the knotting to the nylon below the neck. Use heavy cotton thread and a needle.

Step E.   *Arms*

Prepare the body by lacing up the front, as shown, with a length of doubled #18 cord.

Cut 16 cords of #78 twine, each 9 feet long.

The arms are tubes made of 4 Alternating Square Knots worked in a circle.

Insert the 16 cords through several of the knot openings at the shoulder one row below the top so there are 4 sets of 4 cords grouped for the arm tube (Fig. 4-A).

Begin from each shoulder. Form each arm by tying tightly as follows:

   12 rows Alternating Square Knots
   1 row Reverse Square Knots for elbow
   15 rows Alternating Square Knots

Step F.   *Hands and Fingers*

Cut 10 cords of #18 cotton seine twine, each 6 feet long, for wrapping fingers.

Form Hand:

   Separate cords and tie flat.

   Row 1   4 cords on each side over 8 center cords.

   Row 2   Separate into 2 groups of 8 cords. Use 4 cords for knotting with 4 cords for centers; tie 2 Square Knots.

   Row 3   Tie 3 Square Knots with cords 1 through 4; 7 through 10; 13 through 16. Cords 5, 6, 11, 12 are not used.

   Wrap fingers using 4 cords in 1 finger, 3 cords in 4 fingers, as follows.

HAND KNOTTING CHART

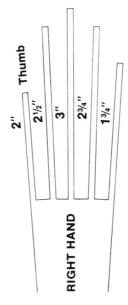

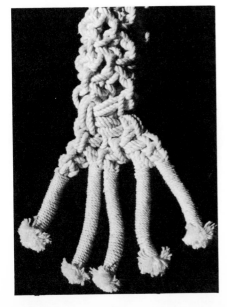

Photo 4-2. Hand detail; use groupings of knots for the hand; wrap ends for the fingers in numbers shown in instructions.

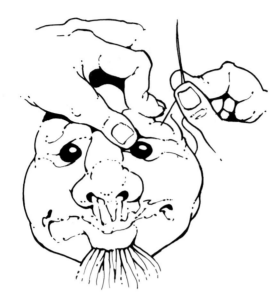

Fig. 4-B. Soft-sculpture face is made by pinching up areas of the stuffed nylon and sewing the features with heavy cotton thread, as shown. Add the eyes and pull through to the back. Actually hold the stuffing as you form the features; the stitching will hold the features in place.

2. PREPARE HEAD, FACE, AND TORSO STUFFED FORM

Finished head size: approximately 7″ high, 6″ wide at cheeks.

Step A.   Stuff a 10″ length of the knee portion of the light-colored nylon stocking with Dacron for the head. For a more wrinkled look, an old cotton T-shirt can be substituted for the Dacron. Old nylons can be used to fill in the center.

Step B.   Shape the head. Tie the stocking at the top and bottom of the head, leaving the loose unstuffed bottom portion for use in the torso.

Step C.   *Face*
The face is made by pinching up portions of the stuffing through the stocking and sewing through the face with a needle and heavy white cotton thread (Fig. 4-B). It is a good idea to stuff a "practice" piece until you get the feel of creating the features. The features are placed in the lower ⅔ portion of the head (see page 91). Begin by pinching up a section for the nose and stitching along the sides, pulling the thread through from one side to the other. Next, pinch up the brow area and sew through; then the mouth. To attach the eyes, use beads and pull the holding threads through to the back of the head and tie tightly so the eyes are indented.

Step D.   *Beard*
Carefully cut a 2″ x 2″ piece of the backing of the fake fur for the beard. Sew to chin, but curve it vertically so it stands away from the chin and fits beneath lower lip.

Step E. *Hair*
   Cut the hair piece 4″ high by 8″ wide and stitch to back of head. Work the loose top portion of the stocking into the head at back, stitch under hair piece to secure.

Step F. *Torso Stuffing*
   Stuff the bottom piece of the stocking to fill the torso, about 11″ long. Shape it so the stomach is wider and thicker than the shoulders (refer to Fig. 4-A). Insert the stuffed portion into the knotted body, adding stuffing as needed. Stitch together at the neck, the bottom of the head, and the top of the torso. Stitch the neck to the top of the macramé at the same time so all parts are secure.
   Lace up the front. Wrap laces' ends to prevent raveling.

Step G. Support head to body if necessary. Sharpen both ends of 12″ wood dowel and insert one end down through gnome's back to about the hips; insert the other end up into back of head.

Step H. *Clothing* (patterns on pages 50–51). Use suede, leather, felt, or wool. Use patterns.
   Hat. Cut to size. Partially fill the hat with stuffing material to fill out and hold shape. Allow the top to fold over for the jaunty look. Stitch edge with doubled thread for an additional detailing through the punched holes. Stitch hat to head, add bell.
   Collar. Cut out. See pattern. Punch holes with a leather or paper punch for design around edge.
   Belt. 12″ long, 1¼″ wide, two 10″ ties. Add buckle on one side.

Clothing:

Fig. 4-D. Belt. Make pattern twice this size (double to 19″)

Place on fold of fabric and cut pattern 15″ long

Fig. 4-C. Hat. Cut pattern twice this size.

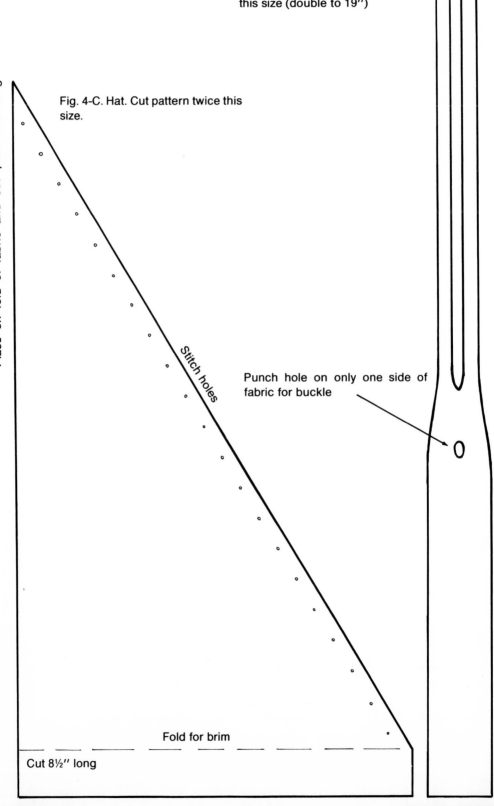

Stitch holes

Punch hole on only one side of fabric for buckle

Fold for brim

Cut 8½″ long

Place on fold of fabric

Fig. 4-E. Collar, actual size

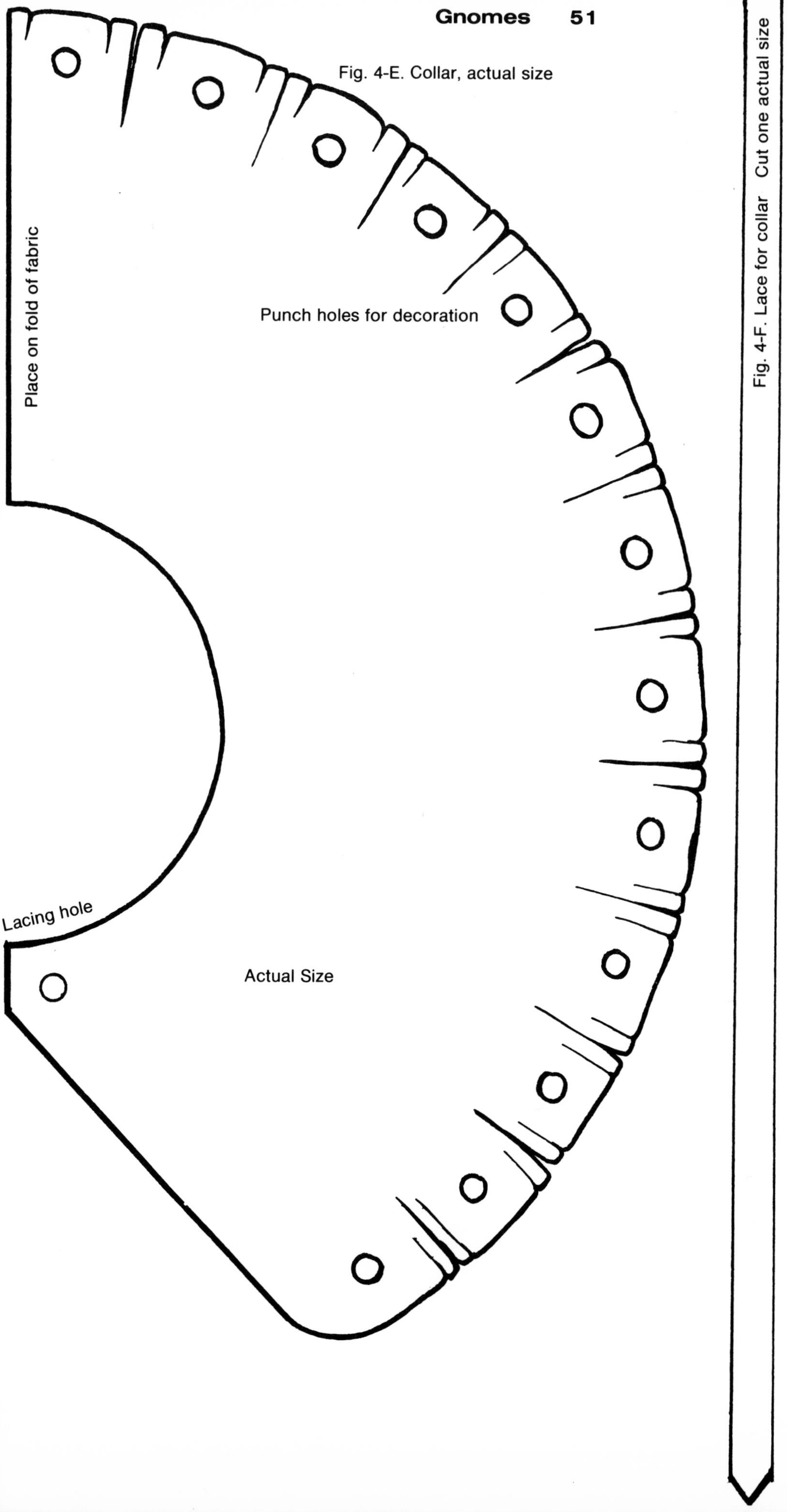

Place on fold of fabric

Punch holes for decoration

Lacing hole

Actual Size

Fig. 4-F. Lace for collar   Cut one actual size

Designer, Bob West

PROJECT 5

MRS. GNOME

Our lovely lady gnome is made essentially the same as her male counterpart but with slight differences in the shaping, features, and, of course, her clothing. The hats use the same patterns, but Mrs. Gnome wears a demure dress and apron; you'll find the patterns on pages 58 and 59. Make her dress and hat of green suede or felt with a brown apron—to offset and complement her rust-brown yarn hair and rich black button eyes.

Materials

187 yards (561 feet) #72 cotton seine twine
  20 yards (60 feet) #18 white cotton seine twine
    1 light-color nylon stocking
    1 package Dacron batting
One 4 oz. skein rust yarn for hair and eyebrows. Use a tightly twisted weaving or knitting yarn of 2mm diameter.
    12" x 26" green suede for dress
    14" x 18" green suede for hat
     7" x 20" brown suede for apron and hat lacing and braid ties
Heavy white cotton thread for sewing
    1 peacock feather
    2 black beads for eyes ⅜" in diameter
Rouge
    1 wood dowel ¼" in diameter and 12 inches long

Tools

Needle for sewing
Punch for making holes in suede
T Pins
Scissors

Finished Size

Top of head to toe: approximately 35 inches.

Instructions

1. KNOTTING

Step A. *Body*

Cut 28 cords of #72 twine, each 20 feet long. Place 12 T pins on a macramé board. Fold 12 cords in half and mount each cord on 1 T pin at the fold to yield 6 sets of knotted cords (4 ends per knot) and tie tightly together. (This begins the upper torso at the neckline.)

BODY KNOTTING CHART
(See Fig. A for shaping)

Key: X = one full Square Knot

|| = unused cords (2 ends)

X = add one double cord (2 ends)

⊗ = add one full Square Knot

Row																	Number of knots
1					X	X	X	X	X	X							6
2					‖ X	X	X	X	X ‖								5
3					X	X	X	X	X	X							6
4			⊗	X	X	X	X	X	X	X	⊗						9
5			‖ X	X	X	X	X	X	X	X ‖							8
6			X	X	X	X	X	X	X	X	X						9
7		⊗	X	X	X	X	X	X	X	X	X	X	⊗				12
8		‖ X	X	X	X	X	X	X	X	X	X ‖						11
9	⊗ X	X	X	X	X	X	X	X	X	X	X	X ⊗					14

Row 10   Remove the holding pins, and tie the 14 Alternating Square Knots in a circle. (The resulting slit in the top torso will be the doll front.)

Row 11   Tie 14 knots around in a circle.

Rows 12–17   Tie 14 knots in a circle in each row, but leave 1″ between knots to allow shape to expand for abdomen.

Rows 18–20   Tie 14 knots in a circle in each row, but tighten to ½″ between knots to shape body in.

Row 21   Tie one row tightly (no space between knots).

Step B. *Legs*
For upper leg: Divide cords in half with 28 working ends in each leg. Tie knots tightly.

Rows 1–9   Tie 7 Alternating Square Knots for each leg.

Row 10   Determine the center back of each leg, and decrease one knot on inside of leg by tying the 4 center back cords in 3 Square Knots (not Alternating). These will drop into the inside of leg and be tucked in and cut off. Tie the remaining cords in 6 Reverse Square Knots to form the knees.

Rows 11–15   Alternating Square Knots in a circle for lower leg.

Row 16   Decrease as in Row 10, and drop center back knot inside leg to shape leg.

Rows 17–22   Tie 5 Alternating Square Knots in a circle to shape for ankle area (20 working ends).

Step C. *Feet*
Follow same illustrations as for Mr. Gnome, page 45, Photo 4-1. For each foot: Separate cords as follows and work toward body front. (The front is where the body is open in Rows 1 to 10.)

SEPARATE GROUPS: 4 cords   12 cords   4 cords

Row 1   Tie the 4 cords at each side in one large Square Knot over the 12 center cords.

SEPARATE GROUPS: 8 cords   4 cords   8 cords

Row 2   Tie one Square Knot at each side, using 8 cords in each. Knot over the 4 center cords.

Rows 3–4   Tie 3 Square Knots with cords divided so there are 4 cords in the center and 8 in each end cord.

Row 5   Begin top of foot with Alternating Square Knots. Counting from left: Tie 2 Square Knots with cords 4 to 8 and 13 to 16 (use 2 center cords for each). The untied end cords will form the top of foot or shoe.
NOTE: For following rows:
Drop 2 end cords from *each row;* these end cords will be used to form shoe top. The sole portion will become narrower.

Row 6   5 Alternating Square Knots (leave the 2 end cords at each end)

Row 7   4 Alternating Square Knots

Row 8   3 Alternating Square Knots

Row 9   4 Alternating Square Knots

Row 10   3 Alternating Square Knots

Row 11   2 Alternating Square Knots

Row 12   3 Alternating Square Knots

Row 13   2 Alternating Square Knots

Row 14   1 Alternating Square Knot

Row 15   2 Alternating Square Knots

Row 16   1 Alternating Square Knot

Step D.   *Top of Foot* (same as Mr. Gnome page 45, Photo 4-1)
Pick up the end cords from Row 5. Use one cord on each side for knotting and the others in the center plus work on top of sole.
Continue in each row, using one each end cord for the knot with the other cords in the center. With each row, the central cords will increase, and this vertical group will become thicker and narrower to form the toe.
Tie last knot very tightly, and insert ends up into foot so it won't loosen. Center cords become toe ends. Unply and fluff out.
Repeat the same knotting progression for the other foot, and be sure to match knot sizes so the feet are the same.

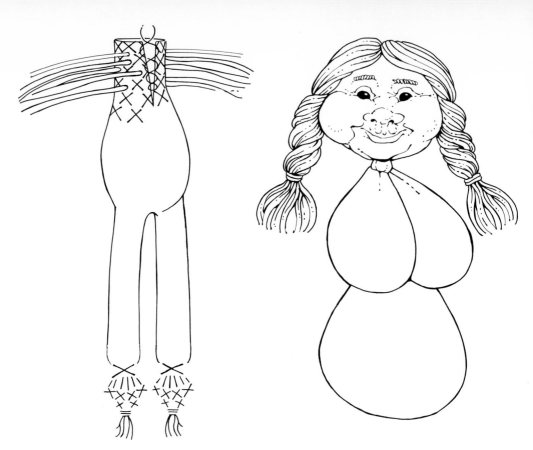

Fig. 5-A. Body shaping and insertion of arms, Step E.

Fig. 5-B. Head and torso construction. See page 48, Fig. 4-B, for creating soft-sculpture face.

Step E. *Arms*

Prepare the body by lacing up the front, as shown, with a length of cord as you would lace a shoe.

Cut 16 cords of #78 twine, each 9 feet long, and insert through body at shoulders, one row below top in a circle as shown in Fig. 5-A. The arms are developed as tubes made of 4 Alternating Square Knots worked in a circle. Begin from each shoulder, and form each arm by tying tightly as follows:

      11 rows Alternating Square Knots
      1 row Reverse Square Knots for elbow
      12 rows Alternating Square Knots

Step F. *Hands and Fingers* (same as Mr. Gnome page 47)

Cut 10 cords of #18 cotton seine twine, each 6 feet long, for wrapping fingers.

Form Hand:

    Separate cords and tie flat.

    Row 1   4 cords on each side over 8 center cords.

    Row 2   Separate into 2 groups of 8 cords. Use 4 cords for knotting with 4 cords for centers; tie 2 Square Knots.

    Row 3   Tie 3 Square Knots with cords 1 through 4; 7 through 10; 13 through 16. Cords 5, 6, 11, 12 are not used.

    Wrap fingers using 4 cords in 1 finger, 3 cords in 4 fingers.

2. PREPARE HEAD, FACE, AND TORSO STUFFED FORM, Fig. 5-B

Head: Top to chin, 6″; outer cheek to outer cheek, 5″.
Neck: 1½″ long.
Chest: 3½″ long, 5″ wide.
Hips: 8″ at widest part.

Step A. Use a light-colored nylon stocking. Stuff a 10″ length of the stocking for the lower torso in a pear shape, as shown. Unlace doll and insert to fill out macramé portion.

Step B. Stuff a 12″ portion for the head and chest in an egg-timer shape. Tie ends. Shape. Tie off top of head and shape.

Step C. *Face*
The face is made by pinching up portions of the stuffing through the stocking and sewing through the face with a needle and heavy white cotton thread. It is a good idea to stuff a "practice" piece until you get the feel of creating the features. Usually the features are placed in the lower ⅔ portion of the head (see page 91).
Begin by pinching up a section for the nose and stitching along the sides, pulling the thread through from one side to the other.
Next, pinch up the brow area and sew through; then the mouth.
To attach the eyes, use beads and pull the holding threads through to the back of the head and tie tightly so they are indented.
Sew on eyebrows with a single strand of the same yarn as used for the hair.

Step D. *Hair*
Cut one whole skein of rust macramé weaving yarn to yield 26″ lengths.
Arrange on head and sew center to head with length of yarn in a needle, using a running stitch.
Begin at ear height, and braid each side for pigtails. Tie with a length of suede lace.
Stitch hair to sides of female gnome's head.

Step E. *Clothing*
Cut dress from green suede. Use a brown suede lace. Pattern: Fig. 5-C (pages 58–59).
Cut apron from brown suede. Pattern: Fig. 5-D.
Cut hat from green suede (same pattern as male gnome, page 50, Fig. 4-C). Stuff lower portion of hat, and stitch to head. Add feather.
Touch the cheeks, chin, nose, and exposed chest lightly with dry rouge.
Sharpen both ends of the wood dowel and insert in gnome's back and head for spinal support.

Fig. 5-D. Apron. Make ties 17 inches each side. Cut apron and dress actual size.

For hat, use the same pattern as for Mr. Gnome, Fig. 4-C, page 50.

Fig. 5-C. Dress. Fold fabric in fourths and place on folds as shown. Cut out circle at front and slit down center front. Make lace holes on both sides of the slit in position shown and lace with a length of suede.

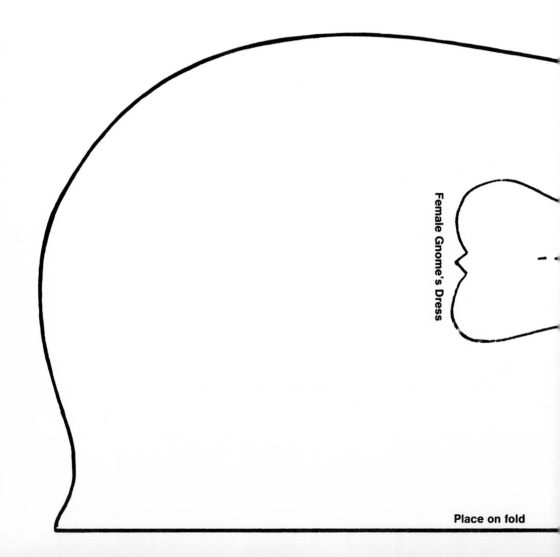

Female Gnome's Dress

Place on fold

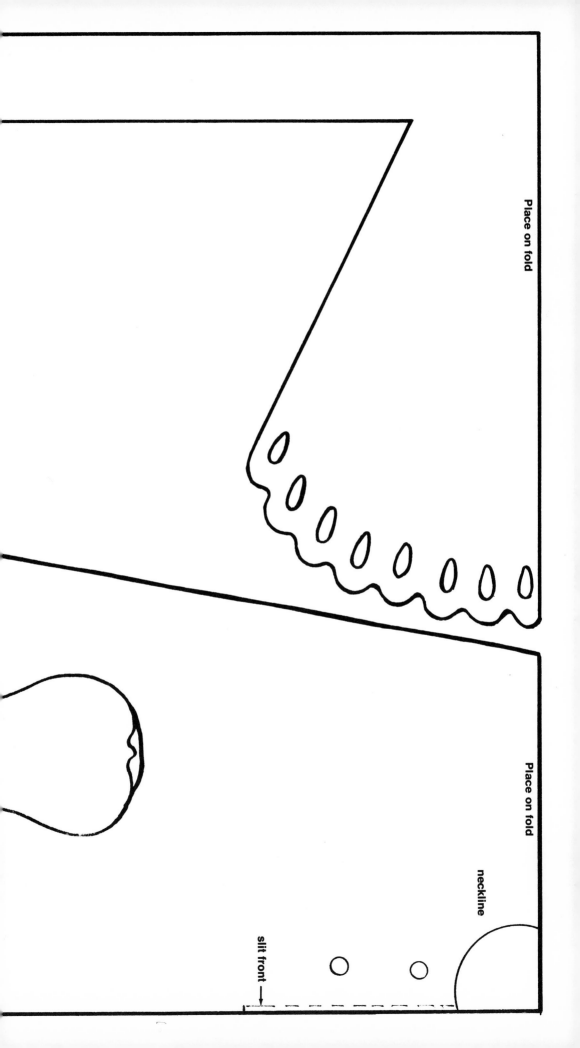

Place on fold

Place on fold

neckline

slit front

Designer, Mary Baughn

PROJECTS 6 AND 7

WOODLAND GNOMES

A gnome can be as imaginative as you dare. Designer Mary Baughn, who had never heard of gnomes before she made these, put her imagination to work on a midwestern cold snowy night and quickly created the friendly beings to keep her company. The basic body is an armature extending from the head and which can be dressed in any costume you like. Begin with Mary's costuming, and learn how easy it is to create macramé clothing. Then design a complete gnome family of your very own to help with the chores around the house, to talk to, or whatever you would like to have them do to make your life more pleasant.

Woodland Gnomes may be used as toys, or with strings attached as puppets that can be manipulated by control boards as in the string puppets (page 26). Attach string to head, wrists, and knees. They can be adapted to hand or sleeve puppets, by attaching a macramé layer at the back and inserting the hand up beneath it: Allow an open knotted space at the back of the head just above the neck to insert a finger.

Materials

Each gnome is made entirely of polypropylene macramé cord ⅛" (3.175mm). (Use Lily Macra-Cord, OR Knot Craft Herculon, OR other similar brand.)

75 yards white for head and armature
100 yards for garments (all red for girl; 50 yards gold and 50 yards blue for boy)
6 yards brown for shoes
30 yards red or blue for hats and details
12 pipe cleaners
Cone-shaped form—1¼" in diameter at top smallest portion
Cardboard tube, ¾" in diameter and about 6" long, OR foamed plastic OR wood dowel

Finished Size

Height, 22 inches.

Instructions

1. PREPARE HEAD AND BODY ARMATURE (see page 68)

    Hat

    Cut 16 red cords each 1½ yards long for beginning at top of hat.

Row 1   Beginning: Interweave 4 cords folded in half as shown (Fig. 6-A, page 63). Place one folded cord within each folded cord of the interweave.

Row 2   Tie one Square Knot with each set of 4 cords; pull the central cords tightly to form peak of hat. Pin cords to top of narrow end of cone.

Rows 3–4   Tie Alternating Square Knots in a circle around cone.

Row 5   Increase: Add 8 cords folded in half evenly around the circumference of the cone. (Square Knot increase, page 14. Tie 8 Alternating Square Knots around cone.

Rows 6–12   Continue to tie Alternating Square Knots around cone, allowing the form to increase in diameter.

Face

Cut 1 ivory cord 6 yards long for face.
Cut 1 blue cord 2 feet long for eyes.
Continue back of head: Tie 5 Alternating Square Knots with red for 7 rows.
For face:

Rows 13–14–15   Tie vertical Clove Hitches over 12 cords from Square Knots at front of hat. At each side, catch the first wrap of the Clove Hitch in Row 13 with the first cord of the Square Knot from the back to secure white and red together. Do the same with the first wrap of Row 15.

Row 16   Add in Eyes. Tie Vertical Clove Hitches with ivory over 3 cords, blue over 2 cords, ivory over 2 cords, blue over 2 cords, ivory over 3 cords.

Ears

Make the ears to be added in with Row 17.
Cut 5 lengths of ivory each 30″ for *each* ear. Use the angled Clove Hitching (Fig. 6-B).
Left Ear:

Row 1   Tie one Overhand Knot in center of cord A.

Row 2   Mount cord B to left of Overhand Knot on A with a Lark's Head and tie each of the resulting 3 vertical strands in a Clove Hitch over half of A held as the horizontal cord. Mount cord C on A with a Lark's Head. Extend cord A at right. All resulting cords that are horizontal will be used to tie ear to head.

Row 3   Add in a 4th cord (length D) as in Row 1 with cord E mounted next to the Overhand Knot.

Rows 4–7   Continue picking up the left-hand cord for each row, extending it horizontally and Clove Hitching the vertical strands, and angle knotting will result. Clove Hitch the remaining cords over horizontals picked up at left; leave all ends extended at right. In each row, there will be one fewer knot with only one knot on the 7th row.
Right Ear:
Repeat as above but work angle from right to left.

Nose

Cut 2 red cords each 2 feet long. Repeat angle knotting as for ears but use only 2 cords A & B for 4 rows.
Continue face:

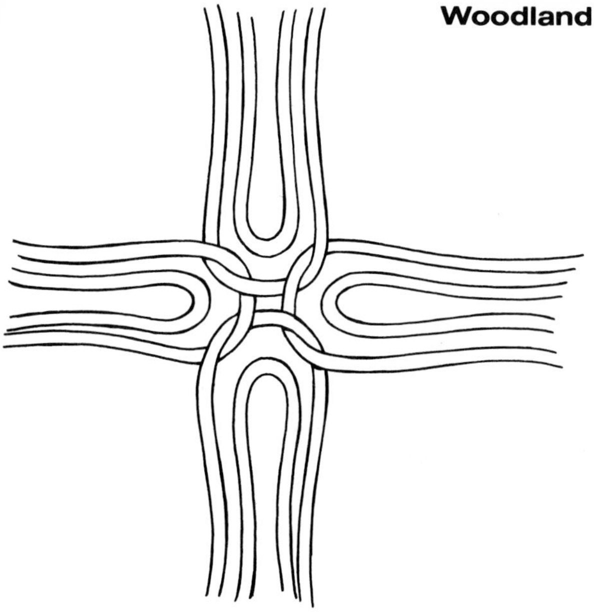

Fig. 6-A. Begin the top of the hat by interweaving 4 cords, then adding another folded cord within each woven cord, as shown. Work over the top pointed circumference of the cone.

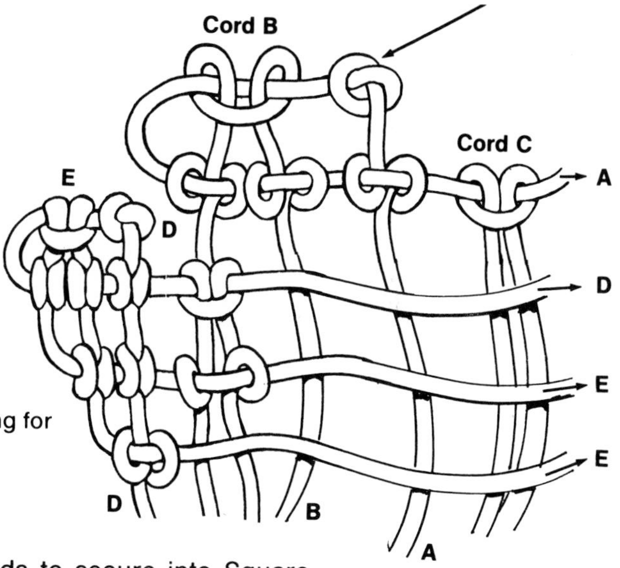

Overhand Knot on Center of Cord A

Cord B

Cord C

Fig. 6-B. Angled Clove Hitching for Ears and Nose.

Row 17 *Insert Ears.* Place ear ends to secure into Square Knots: Pick up ear ends ''A'' from each side and use for one row of Vertical Clove Hitches across face. Do not cut off ends; all loose ends and floating cords should be placed inside head.

Row 18 *Add nose.* Use ivory left ear cords or ivory face cords (whichever is available) and tie 6 ivory Vertical Clove Hitches. Add nose between rows and knots. Pull cords inside head tightly (ends will be used for mouth). Tie 6 more ivory Vertical Clove Hitches across face and secure in the ear cords.

Rows 19–21 Ivory Vertical Clove Hitch across face, using some of the ear cords from each side to secure ears to head. Also catch end knots around Square Knotting at back of head to attach face to head.

Row 22 Add mouth. Tie 3 ivory Vertical Clove Hitches. Hold the ivory cord horizontally. For the upper lip use red cords from nose and tie 6 Horizontal Clove Hitches over the ivory horizontal cord and catch a red vertical cord into each knot. Tie 3 more ivory Horizontal Clove Hitches.

Row 23 Tie 4 ivory Vertical Clove Hitches. Tie 4 red Horizontal Clove Hitches for lower lip as in Row 22. Tie 4 more ivory Vertical Clove Hitches.

Row 24 Remove knotting from cone. Begin to shape chin. Tie ivory Vertical Clove Hitches across face front.

Row 25   Continue to tie Vertical Clove Hitches with ivory across face; then at back of head knot over every other Square Knotted red vertical cord and drop the alternate cord inside the head; this will create a decrease.

Row 26   Decrease all around face and head; knot over 2, drop 1, using the ivory all around.

Row 27   Decrease; tie over 1, drop 1, with ivory all around.

BODY ARMATURE (see page 68)

Neck

Cut a 4-yard length of ivory cord.
Gather all the remaining head cords and use them as the Square Knot fill. Tie the 4-yard ivory cord around the gathered fill cords in 3 Square Knots for neck.

Legs and Arms

Legs—make two. For *each* leg:
Cut 2 brown cords each 1½ yards long.
Cut 1 ivory cord each 4 yards long.
3 pipe cleaners.

Step A.   Work from the toe up: Use 2 brown cords for the shoe, fold 1 brown cord in half and tie an Overhand Knot 20″ from one end. (Same starting procedure as for ears, but *not* on an angle.) Mount another cord onto the short side of the cord and next to the Overhand Knot with a Lark's Head. Work the long end as the holding cord and tie 3 Clove Hitches back and forth for 8 rows.

Step B.   Lay the brown cord ends along 3 pipe cleaners lightly twisted together. Place the 4-yard lengths of ivory cord at shoe top and tie Half Knot Twists for 9½″ over the brown cords and pipe cleaners which serve as the filler cords in the leg.
Arms—make two. For *each* arm you will need:
Cut 1 ivory cord 3 yards long for tying.
Cut 1 ivory cord 1 yard long for filler.
3 pipe cleaners.

Step C.   Work from the fingers up: Fold the 3-yard cord in half and tie 2 Overhand Knots at center. Pin to knotting board.

Step D.   Lay pipe cleaners on board. Fold the tip of one pipe cleaner over the sharp wire ends of the other two. Fold the 1-yard filler cord over the end of the pipe cleaners and press against Overhand Knots of the tying cord. Tie Half Knot Twists with the long cord ends using the pipe cleaners/cord assembly for the filler.

ASSEMBLE ARMS AND LEGS TO BODY

Step A.   Lay the arm ends at front of neck with the wire and all cord ends laid in with the neck filler cords toward bottom of doll. Use the neck knotting cords and continue to make 2 tight Square Knots to secure arms to body.

Step B.   Place top of leg cords along body cords and tie 14 more Square Knots to secure all together: body, arm, and

Woodland Gnome—Girl

Designer, Mary Baughn

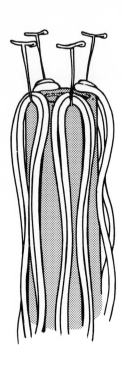

Fig. 6-D. Pin mounting on cardboard tube for beginning sleeves,
and pants at cuffs.

leg cord endings. Knotting from top of neck to crotch should be 3″ and about 1½″ diameter. If body becomes too fat, trim away some of the fill cords before knotting.

Step C. Separate the filler cords into 2 legs. Cut a 2-yard ivory cord for each leg and wrap for 2″ to top of Half Knot Twists.
The body is now ready to be dressed.

2. KNOTTING FOR CLOTHING

Boy's Gold and Blue Body Suit (For Girl's Clothes, see page 67)

The body suit is essentially a tube of Alternating Square Knots. Begin by tying around a 1″-diameter tube. Use a cardboard insert form from the inside of one of the balls of cord or a ¾″-diameter dowel of foamed plastic, white PVC plastic, or wood. Begin at the cuff and sleeves, toward the neck. Then add cords and work the body portion downward directly on the doll.

Sleeves

For each sleeve, cut 8 gold cords each 1½ yards long. Fold in half and mount 2 cords on each of four pins inserted at edge of cardboard tube (16 ends—Fig. 6-D). Tie 15 rows of Alternating Square Knots about 6½″ or enough to match length of arm and allowing the hand to show. Remove knotting from tube and slip over doll's arm. Repeat for the other arm.

Front and Back

Cut 8 gold cords each 1½ yards long. Use 4 cords at the front and 4 at the back.

Rows 1–6 With sleeves on doll, pin 4 cords into doll's body at the front and 4 at the back. Pick up the cords from the sleeves and incorporate garment's front and back cords to yield 10 sets of knotting cords. Work Alternating Square Knots around the doll's body for 2″.

Row 7 Decrease to 8 knots to shape the garment at the waist by dropping the front and back center knotting cords inside the work.

Rows 8–11 Tie 8 sets of Alternating Square Knots around the body. Trim ends of gold cords evenly at top of legs.

Pants

Cut 8 blue cords each 1½ yards long.
Fold in half and mount two cords together around the filler cords of each gold knot in the blouse between the 9th and 10th rows (or 3″ from neck).

Rows 1–6 Tie 9 Alternating Square Knots with blue for pants top (2½″).

Rows 7–27 Separate cords evenly for legs so there are 4 sets of knots in each leg. Tie Alternating Square Knots for 20 rows (7″).

Row 28   Tie an Overhand Knot in each cord as close as possible to the end of the Square Knotting to secure all ends.
Trim ends to about 2″ or even with top of shoe.

Add Necktie

Lace a 24″ length of blue cord through the knots at the
neckline and tie in a bow at the front.

GIRL DOLL

Girl's Blouse

Begin arm and blouse the same as for the boy doll, using
red instead of gold.

Girl's Pants and Skirt

Begin the pants at the cuff over leg armature, then knot a
tube for the skirt as an extension of the pants.
Cut 8 red cords each 3½ yards long for each leg (16 cords
for both legs), fold back for skirt.
Cut 1 red cord 2 feet long.
Begin pants cuffs as for sleeves (Fig. 6-D). Mount 2 cords
on each of 4 pins for each leg.

Rows 1–23   Tie 4 Alternating Square Knots for 23 rows (9½″).
Make two.

Rows 24–29   Tie 8 sets of Square Knots from both legs all
around the body lower torso.

Row 30   Tie the 2-foot red cord loosely around waist with
knot at back. Clove Hitch all the knotting cords around
waistband.

Rows 31–35   Fold cords out and tie 8 rows of Alternating
Square Knots all around waist with about 1″ between
knots so that skirt becomes more lacy looking and stands
away from the body.
Finish ends with an Overhand Knot on each cord as close
to the Square Knots as possible to secure. Tie another
Overhand Knot 1½″ farther down on cord. Trim ends
evenly for skirt fringe.

Girl's Collar—Actual size, Fig. 7-E

Cut 1 gold cord 24″ (holding cord).
Cut 15 gold cords about 8″.
Cut 1 blue cord, 1 gold cord, 1 red cord, each 24″ (knot-
ting cords).

Step A.   Mount 15 gold cords 8″ each onto the 24″ holding
cord with Lark's Head Knots. Pin to knotting board in a
circular shape to fit around doll's neck in a 1½″ diameter.

Step B.   Tie 1 row blue Vertical Clove Hitches, allowing cords
to extend at least 2″ at each end.

Step C.   Repeat for gold and red, as for blue.

Step D.   Tie an Overhand Knot 1″ from the knotting in all cords except the gold holding cord. Trim evenly below knots; fluff ends out with the point of a pin. Tie collar around doll's neck in a bow using the long ends of the gold holding cord. Tie Overhand Knots at end of this cord to prevent unraveling.

Fig. 6-C. Armatures of Woodland Gnomes beneath the clothing. Knotting is accomplished over cardboard or foamed plastic cones and dowels.

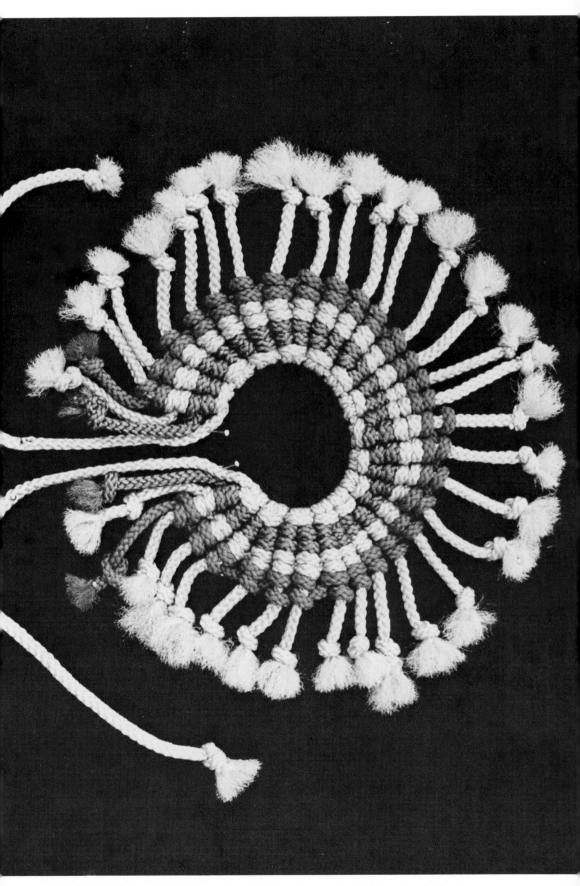

Fig. 7-E. Collar—actual size to fit around neck of girl Woodland Gnome.

Designer, Kathy Browne

PROJECT 8

PETEY, THE PEACOCK PUPPET

Start your own private zoo with furry puppets such as this soft, fluffy, feathery peacock. He can be manipulated along a stage as he is held from below. Your arm extends up into the body and your hand works the control stick. Puppet strings can be attached at the head, the tail flap, along the tail feather ends, and the back so he can be manipulated with string control boards if you prefer. His tail feathers are magnificent when they are spread up high, or allowed to trail along the stage front.

When he is not performing his Thespian role, push stuffing into the body cavity and enjoy his company as he lounges in the corner of a room, propped up on a cushion as a sculpture.

The basic technique for making the peacock involves covering an armature with Spiral Clove Hitches for a "webbing," then knotting short lengths of yarn around the webbing. It is a method that is easily adaptable to any shape in two or three dimensions. The procedure is easy, though the results look complex. Don't let the length of the instructions dismay you. There are several parts to assembling such a big bird but the same basic knots are used throughout. If your knotting results are slightly different from those in the instructions, don't worry about it, as there are infinite ways the cords can be developed around the shapes. Consider the instructions a general guide but feel free to change any of the shapes or relationships of parts to one another.

An entire menagerie in three dimensions would be easy to create by this technique. Use your imagination for animal shapes . . . they need not be true to life; animals in illustrated children's books can be a source of inspiration. If true-to-life forms are those you like, consult books and magazines with photographs of animals published by natural history museums and zoos, and in encyclopedias.

Petey the Peacock shown has the blue-green coloring from which the color "peacock blue" is derived. It is also the male who has the beautifully plumed, elongated upper tail covered with spots touched with iridescent gold and green colors.

Materials

NOTE: Satisfactory results can be achieved using any yarns similar to those suggested. We recommend purchasing a spool of a given color rather than exact yardage as no two people will use the same amounts of cords when adding the fluffy tie-on knotted pieces. Generally, use a jute or other unstretchy cord for the underwebbing. For the fluffy tie-on cords, use a soft 4- to 5mm-thick polyolefin indoor-outdoor cable cord because it is easy to unply the ends, it will not unravel, and a thick cord will fill up space quickly. Except for the beak detail, avoid using slippery nylon cords that untie and unravel readily. You may already have scraps of some colors that can be used for color detailing. Think of simulating the colors of the real bird by mixing the yarn colors on the back, on the chest, on the head, just as a painter mixes color on his canvas. Spool amounts may differ by manufacturer. Use your judgment when purchasing, with the following as your guide:

MACRAMÉ CORDS

100 yards medium-blue jute, 5 ply, 5mm (for webbing)

One 72-yard spool turquoise polyolefin indoor-outdoor cable cord 4.3mm

Two 48-yard spools teal-blue polyolefin indoor-outdoor cable cord 4.3mm

One 48-yard spool emerald-green polyolefin indoor-outdoor cable cord 4.3mm

One 48-yard spool yellow polyolefin indoor-outdoor cable cord 4.3mm

15 yards ivory polyolefin indoor-outdoor cable cord 4.3mm

6 yards white nylon or other shiny cord 3mm for beak detail only

Embroidery floss—2 skeins radiant blue, 1 skein bright gold or yellow

ALSO

3 lengths 20-gauge floral wire each 20″ long for antennae

Two 1″-diameter blue glass buttons for eyes

Three rings, one 4″, one 6″, and one 7″ in diameter

2 foamed plastic eggs, one 6″ for head, one 10″ to 12″ (approximately) for body, OR build up shape from layers of foam, OR work over a basket or shaped cardboard

1 wood dowel ¾″ in diameter and 18″ long

1 old umbrella frame with at least 7 ribs intact for bird's tail
OR
A 1″ ring and seven 12- to 16-gauge wire rods each 20″ long

White glue

Wooden crochet hook

Yarn needle with large eye

Masking tape

Wire cutter

T pins

Plastic bristle hairbrush to use for hair blowing

Finished Size

Head to tail: approximately 37 inches long.

Fig. 8-A. Step 1-A Beginning the beak and the foot. Fold one cord and make an Overhand Knot at the fold. Clove Hitch one side onto the other.

Fig. 8-B. Step 1-B Attach the beak pin to foamed plastic ball. Mount a white nylon holding cord A around beak. Mount 3 additional white cords around the top of A. These mountings will form detail of the mouth area.

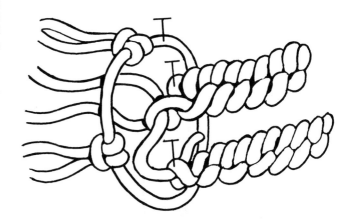

Instructions

HEAD

1. Beak and Nostrils

Cut 2 gold cords each 30″ long for the *beak*. Use one cord for the upper beak and one cord for the lower beak.

Step A. For each beak: (Fig. 8-A) Fold one cord in half. Make an Overhand Knot in center. Use one half of the cord for the anchor; use the other half to tie Clove Hitches over the anchor. Tie the beaks together at the end with a Clove Hitch from the bottom beak around the three other cords.

Cut 7 white nylon cords, each 36 inches long, for the *nostrils*.

Step B. Thread one length through the last knot of the beak. Secure beak and 1 white nylon cord (a) to tip of 6″ foamed plastic egg (Fig. 8-B). Mount 3 white cords doubled onto each side of the white nostril cord with a Lark's Head. The Lark's Heads form the nostril; they should be pushed together tightly. All the ends will be used for the head webbing made with the Spiral Clove Hitch.

2. Crown (Fig. 8-C, Step 2)

Use 3 lengths of floral stem (or similar gauge wire) each 20″ long. Cut 21 lengths of teal-blue cord each 7″ long, for each plume of crown.

Step A. Mount 7 cords at the center of one length of floral wire with Lark's Head Knots. Bunch cords together tightly and fold wire in half. Pinch the loop and twist the wires together to about 1″ from ends.
Unply and fray ends of strands for feathery look.

Step B. Use teal-blue 6-strand embroidery floss and tightly wrap around the twisted wires. Secure ends under wrapping and trim off.
Repeat for other 2 wires to make total of 3 plumes.
Set aside until head webbing is finished.

3. Eyes

Use two buttons about 1″ diameter with a loop shaft. String buttons onto a piece of doubled embroidery floss and pin into position. When working the webbing for the

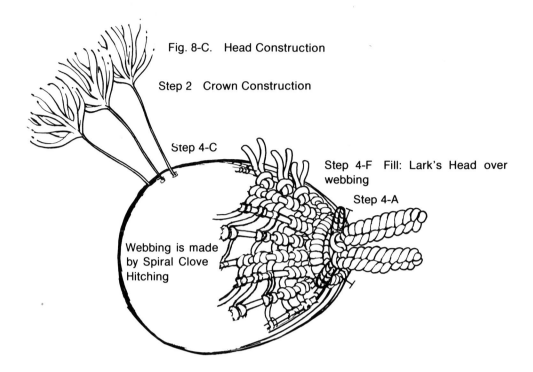

Fig. 8-C.   Head Construction

Step 2   Crown Construction

Step 4-C

Step 4-F   Fill: Lark's Head over webbing

Step 4-A

Webbing is made by Spiral Clove Hitching

head, tie the eyes securely onto a cord and work the ends of the thread into the knotting.

4.   Webbing and Fill for Head (Fig. 8-C)

Cut 12 turquoise-blue cords each 5 feet long.
Cut one blue holding cord 20″ long.

Step A.   Pin blue holding cord around front of egg at edge of and under nostril and beak. Mount 8 blue cords evenly around holding cord. Tie all available blue and white cords evenly around egg with the Spiral Clove Hitch knot with about ¾″ between each knot. (Incorporate the ends from the nostril mounting.) Secure the blue holding cord to the white nostril cord by stitching together with white embroidery floss.

Step B.   As the spaces between the knots increase (about the 6th row), add 4 more doubled cords along the top to expand the shape and keep the webbing close together. Continue knotting all cords and work so the ends develop toward the bottom of the egg that will become the neck. Incorporate the threads that hold the eyes.

Step C.   Insert wire endings from plumes in top of head; make a small hole in the foamed plastic egg. Add white glue into hole; insert wires; add more glue if necessary.

Fill: (Fig. 8-D)

Step D.   Cut the following colors into 6″ lengths, for the fill for the head: 12 emerald green for back of head; 80 lengths of turquoise for all around head; 18 ivory for around eyes; 18 dark blue for chin and center of forehead. Tie each length onto the webbing cords with Lark's Head Knots, pushing them close together so they look like cut pile carpeting. To insert fill cords where webbing is far apart, un-ply some of the web cords and insert the fill lengths between the plies as needed. Cords may be pulled under the webbing with a wooden crochet hook.

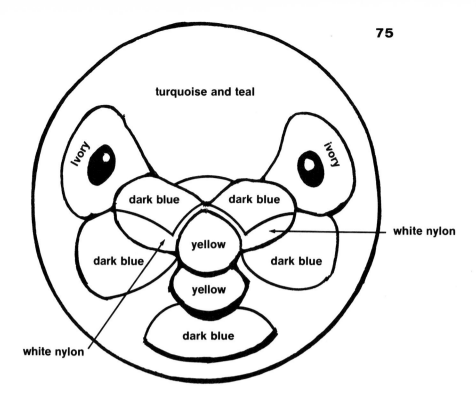

Fig. 8-D.   Color pattern for head fill

Step E.   When head is completely filled in, gather all the web cord ends together and insert through the 2″ metal ring. Push 2″ neck ring up (Fig. 8-E) to base of egg in position shown in photo of peacock, page 70.

   5.   *Neck and Body* (Fig. 8-E)

Step A.   Mount 12 green cords each 72″ long for body webbing. Mount around the 2″ ring at the neck base with a Lark's Head. Separate the cords into groups of 4 and twist or braid so they will be out of way temporarily.

Step B.   Secure the ring under the head at the neck base by tying it on with the head webbing cords at about 8 places around the ring. Tie off all the ends tightly with Square Knots. Trim ends.

Step C.   Shape a 6″ foamed plastic egg (or other form) to the general shape of the bird's body. Flatten the point of the egg. Flatten one side for the top, or back, of the bird by pressing on a flat surface (page 38, Fig. 3-A). A body shape can also be made from layers of foam sheet glued or taped together and formed to the necessary size, approximately 6″ in diameter and 13″ long. Push the small end of the egg inside the 2″ ring. Unbraid the green cords and work them around the body with the Spiral Clove Hitch to make the webbing, as for the head.
   In Rows 5, 10, and 15, increase with 4 cords at the bottom or "abdomen" of the figure; knot these increases back and forth over the abdomen to expand the shape; do not work them entirely around the form. Knot an extra row of these back and forth in each 3rd row of the front to one row of the back so shaping is gradual.

Step D.   Work the webbing for approximately 5″. Add a 6″ metal ring around the center of the body; tie in by a row of horizontal Clove Hitching with each cord around the ring. Tie Spiral Clove Hitches for 5 more inches.
   NOTE: The foamed plastic form can remain in the figure if

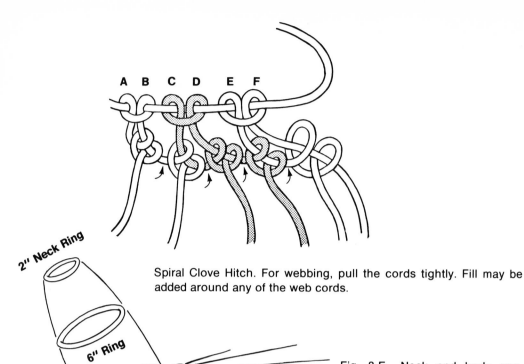

A B C D E F

2" Neck Ring

6" Ring

7" Ring

Spiral Clove Hitch. For webbing, pull the cords tightly. Fill may be added around any of the web cords.

Fig. 8-E. Neck and body construction. Rings are knotted in for support at the neck, center, and bottom of body.

the peacock will be used as a sculpture or pillow. It may be removed and the body stuffed with a softer material such as polyurethane stuffing, rags, or nylon hose. If the bird will be used as a puppet, remove the form and insert a wood dowel 18″ long and ¾″ in diameter up into the body and secure it into the "egg" head on a slight angle. Secure well with white glue. Place tape over the bottom end of the dowel for easier handling while you complete the figure.

Step E.   Separate 24 cords at bird's back. Half of these will be used for the tail flap and half for securing the tail-feather armature. Tie the remaining front cords around the 7″ ring with horizontal Clove Hitches and secure by tying every pair together with a Square Knot. Trim to 1½″ and unply.

Step F.   Fill in bird's body with 6″ lengths of yarn tied onto the webbing with the Lark's Head Knots in the approximate areas and color schemes: 60 lengths of emerald green in an elongated diamond shape on the back with the point at the top center of neck. 80 lengths of dark blue for chest and bottom front. 150 lengths turquoise overall.

6.   Tail Feather Armature (Fig. 8-F)

Step A.   The wire tail armature can be made from an old umbrella frame (try a secondhand shop if you don't have one). Use 7 ribs on one side of the cord.
OR:
Fashion an armature by using a 1″-diameter metal ring. Attach 7 heavy pieces of 14-gauge wire 20″ long for the ribs. Bend one end over ring. Wrap ring with emerald-green cord about 24″ long and bring two winds of the wrapping between each rib with all the ends placed on one half of the ring.

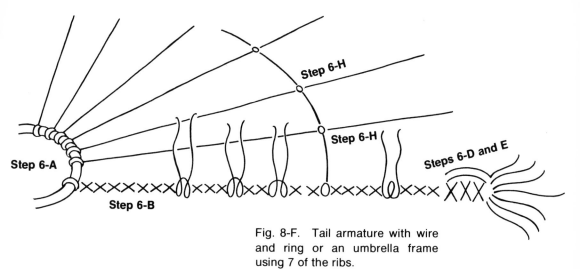

Fig. 8-F. Tail armature with wire and ring or an umbrella frame using 7 of the ribs.

Step B. For knotting on *each* rib (you will need 7 ribs and *one* set of the following *for each rib*):

1 dark-blue cord 10 yards	1 turquoise cord 15″
26 turquoise cords each 12″	1 emerald-green cord 15″
6 dark-blue cords each 12″	1 dark-blue cord 15″
2 gold cords each 4 feet	1 dark-blue cord 6″

Fold the 10-yard dark-blue cord in half around the rib top. Use the rib itself as the core and tie Square Knots for 4″ with the blue cords over the rib.

Step C. Tie one Overhand Knot in the center of each 12″ turquoise and each 12″ dark-blue cord. Place the knot on the bottom of the rib with one end at each side of the rib. Bring the ends up and catch them under the dark-blue Square Knotting for one knot only. Lift the cord ends up to become the "feathers." Tie two Square Knots between each "feather" cord. Add the cords as follows: Begin with 1 dark blue, 7 turquoise, a dark blue, and continue adding the dark blue with the turquoise. (Change the relationship of dark blues to turquoise on each rib so they are not all exactly the same.) Unply and comb out the ends of the added feather cords. Continue to 1½″ from end of rib.

Step D. Finish rib ending with a Square Knot button. Place 2 folded lengths of gold over the blue Square Knotting cord. Use *one* gold cord at each side and Square Knot over the 2 gold and the 2 blue filler cords (NOT over the rib), tie 5 Square Knots.

Step E. Lay the 15″ turquoise, emerald-green, and dark-blue cords together and tie them in one Overhand Knot at the middle. Lay the knot perpendicularly on the Square Knot-ted rib ending; it becomes the center and stuffing for the button. Finish the button by bringing the filler cords up and around through the top knot (5 knots up), then secure all cords by tying a Square Knot with the gold knotting cord. Unply and fluff out all ends.

Step F. Secure the colored strands by tying the 6″ length of blue around the ends protruding through the button. Tie these beneath the button in a tassel fashion. Repeat for remaining 6 ribs.

Step G. Secure tail to bird (Fig. 8-G). Untie the reserve lengths of yarn from the back. Pick up every other cord and use 12 cords. Bring them OVER the 7" ring and through the 2" tail armature ring. Place two strands between each rib to help keep the ribs separated and secure. Gather the 12 ends together and tie in 2 large Overhand Knots close to the ring and so they won't slip through. Unply and brush out all cord endings after trimming to about 2".

Step H.   The ribs should open and close to simulate the real train of the peacock tail. To prevent the ribs from falling apart all the way, and to control spacing, cut 6 lengths of 14" turquoise cord and tie one between each rib so ribs are spread 10" apart. Tie spacer cords 8" from the rib end (Fig. 8-F, Step 6-H).

7. Tail Flap

Step A.   For the tail flap webbing, tie vertical Clove Hitches close together over the 12 remaining cords at the back tail end. Cut an 8-yard length of emerald green and develop the tail shape shown for the flap:

Row 1   Vertical Clove Hitch over two cords together 6 times

Row 2   Over 2 cords together, over 8 individual cords, over 2 cords together

Row 3   Over 1 cord for 12 knots

Row 4   Increase: Cut 2 lengths of emerald green each 20". Fold in half and insert between rows 4 and 5 and 8 and 9. Knot across 16 cords.

Row 5   Over 1 cord for 16 knots

Rows 6–15   Gradually decrease to make the diamond shape by knotting over end pairs of cords, then over 3 cords at a time. Toward bottom, knot over 3 cords at a time in center, then cut off ends so shape will gradually come to a point and only 3 cords remain. The entire tail flap should measure about 10" long and 9" wide at widest point.

Step B.   Fill in with about 150 lengths of 6" emerald-green cords tied with Lark's Head Knots onto the Clove Hitched webbing.

Step C.   Run a 24" length of emerald-green cord, in a needle, around the outer edge of the diamond shape and pull the cord slightly until the tail flap forms a gentle curve over the top of the tail feather armature.

8. Feet

For each foot, cut 4 gold cords each 4 feet long.

Step A.   Tie an Overhand Knot at the center of each cord (same as for beak) and use one cord doubled for each toe of the foot. Tie Lark's Head chain knots so they lie flat as follows:
   a.   One cord with 5 knots for center toes
   b.   Two cords with 4 knots for side toes
   c.   One cord with 2 knots for heel of foot

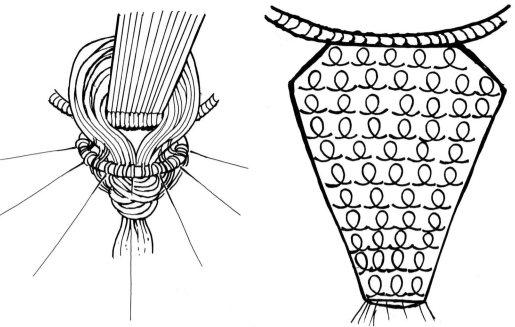

Fig. 8-G. Step 6-G Secure tail to bird by bringing half of the cords at the back of the body through the ring and tying in a gathered Overhand Knot. The remaining cords will be used to knot the tail flap.

Fig. 8-H. Step 7-A Tail flap construction and shaping

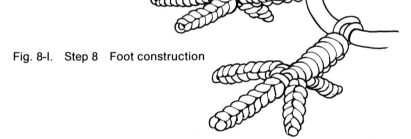

Fig. 8-I. Step 8 Foot construction

Arrange 6 ends (Figure 8-I) of other toes along heel cords and bind 7 ends together with the knotting cord for 5 more Lark's Head chains. Repeat for other foot.

Step B. Anchor feet to ring at front of bird at each side. Carry the last chain of the foot around the 7″ ring and tie onto ring. Secure with an Overhand Knot. Stitch with embroidery floss to secure knotting to ring.

Grooming

Trim the yarn ends at different lengths to simulate bird feathers:

Feathers on the *front of the face* are shorter than on top of the head and around neck.

Leave all *body feathers* as long as possible, just trimming as necessary to even them up.

After trimming (or if your bird molts) additional cords can be pulled through the webbing with a crochet hook and tied on.

Fluff out and unply ends by unraveling with your fingers, then brush with a plastic brush whose bristles are wide-spaced.

Designer, Pattie Frazer

PROJECT 9

INDIAN MAIDEN HAND PUPPET

An easy-to-make hand puppet can serve as the prototype for a variety of characters. It is simply a head with a tubular dress tied around the neck. Slits at each side of the dress and an open base allow the hand to manipulate the puppet; the fingers simulate the arms. A gloved hand or a hand cover made of felt or other fabric can be coordinated with the colors of the puppet's clothes.

When you work a hand puppet, the index finger is inserted into the head; the thumb and middle finger become the arms. Many puppeteers wear long sleeves that match the glove so that none of the arm is exposed should the puppet walk above stage level.

A hand-puppet stage is usually high so the puppeteers can duck down behind the stage wall; this is the exact opposite of the type of stage required for string puppets. A string-puppet stage looks more like a real stage in a theater with a high top facade that serves as cover for the standing puppeteers.

The dress pattern for the Indian Maiden hand puppet is made of Alternating Square Knots. It can be redesigned in any pattern you like; a row of Horizontal Clove Hitches could be added for a belt line. Buttons and embroidery can be added to the macramé.

This simple approach for making a hand puppet is offered as a springboard for your own ideas for characters and clothing.

Materials

80 yards gold nylon seine twine, 2mm
20 yards brown yarn for braid, 1mm
 1 yard white satin ribbon ¼" wide
Head—Cut from a gourd 4¼" high, 3½" in diameter; OR a foamed oval or round. Push hole up into center of foam for finger; OR a premade head from a hobby shop.
Flesh-tint acrylic paint; dark-brown acrylic paint for hair and eyes; red for lips; pink for cheeks (or mix a touch of red into flesh tint)
Paintbrush
White glue
Fabric for glove or sleeve—two 10" squares of felt or heavy cotton

Finished Size

Head to bottom of fringe, 25".
Macramé portion, 7" long by approximately 5" wide.

Instructions

1. HEAD

Prepare and paint according to pattern (Fig. 9-A). Braid: Cut 18 lengths of brown cotton twist cord each 3 feet long. Use 6 strands in each of 3 groups and braid from the center out to the ends. About 4" from each end, add in ½ yard white ribbon. Fold ribbon in half and work in with the braid. Tie 9" lengths of ribbon around loose cords at each end for a pigtail hairdo. Trim cords evenly. Arrange the braid back and forth on the head and glue into place.

2. KNOTTING

Dress: Cut 48 lengths of gold cord each 5 feet.
Cut 1 length of gold cord 18" for holding cord.

Step A.   Double and mount 48 knotting cords onto holding cord with Lark's Heads and work in a circle over any 5"-diameter form such as a roll of paper toweling or cardboard tube or foamed plastic cylinder.

Step B.   Tie Alternating Square Knots for 4 rows.

Step C.   Divide cords in half with open, unknotted sections at sides for fingers to protrude. Knot front and back sections separately for 4 rows.

Step D.   Work knots all around connecting the front and back panels for 17 rows or until body measures 7" of knotting. Allow fringe to extend about 5 more inches. Trim evenly. Total body length is 12".

Step E.   Tie holding cord tightly around doll's neck with the arm slits placed at the sides.

3. TO MANIPULATE

Insert gloved hand into doll with index finger in the head, thumb and middle finger for the arms. Make a felt cover for the hands from the pattern given (Fig. 9-B).

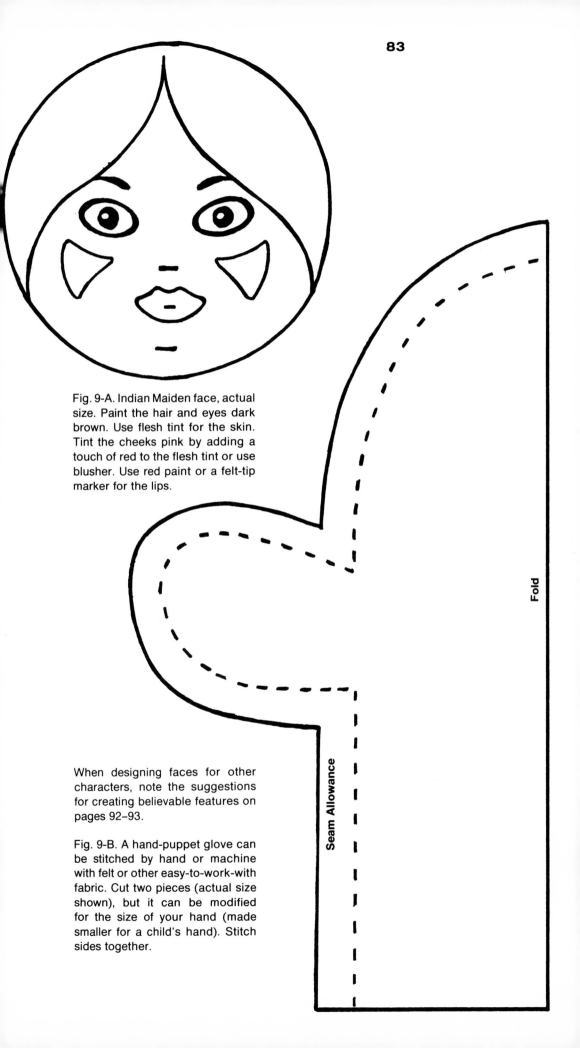

Fig. 9-A. Indian Maiden face, actual size. Paint the hair and eyes dark brown. Use flesh tint for the skin. Tint the cheeks pink by adding a touch of red to the flesh tint or use blusher. Use red paint or a felt-tip marker for the lips.

When designing faces for other characters, note the suggestions for creating believable features on pages 92–93.

Fig. 9-B. A hand-puppet glove can be stitched by hand or machine with felt or other easy-to-work-with fabric. Cut two pieces (actual size shown), but it can be modified for the size of your hand (made smaller for a child's hand). Stitch sides together.

Fold

Seam Allowance

PROJECT 10

CLOWNING AROUND AND OTHER FIGURES

The variety of puppets that can be made with simple macramé knotting over a form is infinite. The clown, opposite, center, is essentially a ready-made head, complete with face and hair with a flared portion at the neck. Assorted ready-made heads are available in craft shops. They are usually sold for doll making but are equally well adapted to puppets.

It is easy to fashion macramé outfits that will fit the heads. The holding cord for the macramé becomes the string that attaches the garment to the head. In this way the garment and head can be interchanged among a variety of puppet characters. Heads are available in sizes from about a 2″ to an 8″ diameter.

Create the clothing by mounting enough cords to fit around the doll's neck onto a holding cord. Work the knotting over a cone or other shape. Allow slits in the clothing so the figure can be used as a hand puppet. If the hand will be inserted from the bottom of the garment leave a slit on each side for the thumb and finger. If you prefer to work the puppet from the back rather than the bottom, leave a slit in the knotting at the back of the garment. Working a hand puppet from the back enables you to make the figure sit more easily on a stage front or over a table edge.

The garment on the clown puppet is made by Spiral Clove Hitching; but any combination of knots may be used. A garment made on the same principle as those in the Woodland Gnomes could also be interchanged with different heads and used as hand puppets. The armature would be eliminated.

Develop your own combinations for colors, for types of cords, for clothing and knot combinations. Add buttons or beads for more detailing that would be in keeping with the figure used.

A practical working method is to pin the neck flare of the head onto the top of the cardboard or foamed plastic cone, or other form. Tie and pin the holding cord with enough knotting cords mounted to it; then begin to knot. You can easily observe the relationship of the clothing to the head size.

If a head has too small a flared neckline for holding a macramé cord, insert a cork into the neck and a piece of hanger wire into the cork; then put the hanger wire into the cone from the top down. The head will sit on top of the cone and make it easier for you to develop the garment. Make a cardboard collar for the head (page 35) to the necessary size. Improvise the method for attaching the collar to the head depending upon how the head is formed. You may have to knot a clothing collar similar to the one in the Woodland Female Gnome (page 69) to camouflage the neck attachment, or cut a collar from felt or Craft Fur. Use your creative ingenuity so that the functional attachments become decorative as well.

Working with Foamed Plastic

Foamed plastic (Styrofoam® is one brand name) is a basic material for puppetry. It is available in a variety of shapes including balls, cones, pyramids, ovals, and eggs of different sizes, flat sheets about ½″ to 2″ thick, rods, circles, and so forth. It is lightweight, easy to work with, and versatile.

Foamed plastics may be used as forms for macramé shapes—heads, bodies, and so forth. They need not retain their original shape: They can be easily remolded by several techniques.

1. A round ball can be given flat planes by pressing a side against a flat surface.

2. "Shelves" can be created in the foam by pushing the foamed plastic against the edge of a table; it is a good technique for creating cheeks on a face.

3. Pieces can be butted together by gluing and/or pinning one shape to another for noses, bulbous cheeks, ears, hands, fingers, and so forth. Use white glue or acrylic medium to adhere. The additions can be further shaped by compressing them with your fingers or by pushing them against a flat or slightly curved surface depending upon the shape you need.

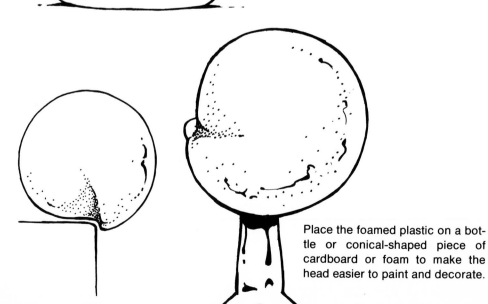

To shape a foam ball or oval to another shape for a head or body, press the foamed form against a flat hard surface. This compresses the cells of the foam.

Place the foamed plastic on a bottle or conical-shaped piece of cardboard or foam to make the head easier to paint and decorate.

A ledge for cheeks is made by pressing the shape against the sharp edge of a desk or table.

4. They may be covered with papier-mâché, fabrics dipped in glue, or pre-glued fabrics.

5. Holes can be easily made in foamed plastic by pushing a sharpened dowel rod or wood pencil through the material. No other tools are required.

For cutting sharp, clean lines, a special low-heat cutter is made. There are also foam-cutting knives and wire tools sold in craft supply shops. But a sharp knife will often serve as well. Small, thin pieces can be cut with a scissors. The foam may be placed in the freezer compartment of a refrigerator for a few hours before cutting; that makes the material hard and easier to cut.

Papier-Mâché and Fabric-Draping Procedures

An unending variety of puppetry heads and details can be made using papier-mâché procedures. Paper scraps and fabric may be used for covering a form. Draping glue-saturated fabric often results in a more natural look for facial and body characteristics than do torn paper scraps, but the procedure for using paper or cloth is essentially the same.

1. Dip the paper or cloth into white glue or acrylic matte medium and adhere to a shaped piece of foamed plastic. Before the materials dry, additional glue medium can be brushed onto the surface to help mold the fabric or paper for details, for wrinkles, and to help make the surfaces adhere to one another. Dry thoroughly.

2. Cover the surface with gesso (depending upon the materials and the look desired). Gesso provides a plain white permanent surface on which to paint details. Dry thoroughly.

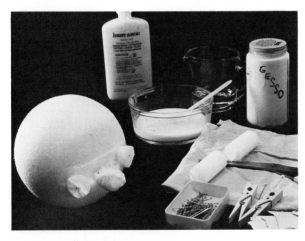

Pin or glue the facial (or other shapes) to one another; press the foamed plastic where necessary for facial contours. You will also need pins, scraps of fabric or paper, scissors, clothespins for holding fabric or other parts of the features together, white glue or acrylic medium, gesso, paint, water, and brushes.

Dip the fabric in the glue or acrylic medium and place it over the foamed plastic. Pin the fabric into place around the added pieces. Push pins in with end of clothespin.

Any portions that have not thoroughly adhered can be further glued by brushing the fabric or paper surfaces with the medium. The brows and some wrinkles have been made with the fabric folds.

When the form is thoroughly dry (overnight or longer) a coat of gesso is applied over the entire piece. It will dry thoroughly in a few hours and yield a hard, chalky surface. The gesso may be tinted if a flesh color is desired. But any color can be applied over the hard, dry gesso coat.

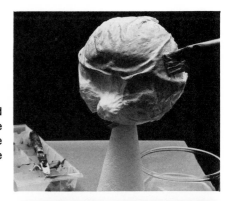

Begin to paint the skin color and add facial coloring. For a skin tone mix a dab of chrome red to white acrylic paint (or other water-base paint).

Begin to think of the features and the hair. Hair is cut from Craft Fur. Always make a pattern, and cut the Craft Fur from the back and only through the backing; then pull the hairy portion apart. You can give the figure a haircut later.

Try craft eyes or paint in eyes. Craft fur, gently separated with the fingers, creates the hair, beard, and moustache. If it is to be permanent, it may be glued, then trimmed; or it can be held on only with pins. Glasses can be fashioned from a length of floral wire and wire bending pliers.

3. Color faces with acrylics, paint, or temperas. Add eyes, eyebrows, and so forth. Finish with a matte or semimatte craft sealer or varnish.

4. Add details of real materials such as Craft Fur, or yarn for hair, beards, and moustaches.

Use the heads on top of macramé bodies. Integrate them with collars or by attaching portions of the fabric into the bodies. The heads may be completely interchangeable depending upon how you form the body. A body made on a dowel rod for shoulders can easily be interchanged by tying on different heads.

The same procedures may also be used for making feet and hands that are not developed directly in the knotting.

The foamed plastic shapes are usually lightweight enough to be used for string puppets. If a head is to be used for a finger puppet, it will be necessary to impress a hole in the neck to use for manipulating it with the finger or with a dowel rod.

When fabric or papier-mâché is built up around a solid form it is possible to remove the inner shape. Let the mache dry completely, then slice through the mache coating and all around it (similar to taking an egg from a whole eggshell by splitting the shell through the circumference). Remove the inner form. Put the two mache parts together by layering mache around the cut until the piece is whole again. It is a marvelous "surgical" technique for creating solid looking, sturdy, but lightweight shapes for puppet heads. It is a practical inexpensive method for developing a wild variety of human, animal, and outrageously imaginative figures for your very own puppetry presentations.

Preparing Gourds

Gourds are used for the puppet heads and hands in Projects 1, 2, and 9. The gourd, a product of nature, is the hard-shelled fruit of a gourd plant; it is sometimes called a "calabash" or a "calabaza." Gourds are grown in many countries, and through the years they have served an infinite variety of utilitarian and decorative purposes. In many primitive cultures a gourd functions as a vessel and utensil, a musical instrument, a basket, or a rattle. Portions of gourds become hair combs, jewelry, scoops; the list is endless.

Pattie Frazer created her clown and Indian Maiden puppets using portions of gourds and it seemed so "natural." It was surprising to realize that contemporary books on gourdcraft do not show them in this context. Dolls, yes, but puppet parts, no. If this is a first, we are happy to introduce it here; though it is possible that some artisan in some far-off country had the same idea.

The marvelous aspect of gourds is that they have the same working characteristics as wood, but the shapes are more natural to figure forms without intricate carving or cutting. Once a gourd is dried (the procedures are described below) it can be sanded, incised, glued, painted, burned, stained, and waxed. If you have a head size or shape in mind, scout around for a gourd that will serve the purpose and you will be delighted with the results.

Where do you find gourds? In the fall, at gourd harvest time, you will find assorted sizes, shapes, and textures of ornamental gourds in your grocery store, hobby shop, nursery, farmer's markets, or gourd farms. Before you chase around looking for them, consult possible suppliers by checking possible listings in your Yellow Pages; then telephone before you make the trip.

It is possible to grow gourds from seed; plant them in April or May when the ground is warm. Seed packets are available where garden supplies are sold. Follow package directions for your area and for soil and growth procedures.

To prepare gourds for puppet heads:

1.   Select a gourd that suggests the head you visualize. Think of how you will cut the round or oval part of the gourd to yield the head and collar shape. Remaining portions can be used for hands, shoes, buttons, and other details.

2.   Gently wash the whole gourd with soapy water and a soft cloth or brush. Wipe dry, place it on paper, and allow it to dry thoroughly in a cool, airy place for three to four weeks. The shell will become hard and you will hear the seeds rattle inside when you shake it. The gourd will be very lightweight because the moisture has dried out from it.

3.   For the head shape, cut portions of the gourd with any saw used for woodworking. Remove seeds and fibrous materials from the inside and clean it out with fine steel wool if necessary. Sandpaper, very carefully, any mold spots on the outside and the cut edge. Drill necessary holes for stringing through the puppet with a small diameter wood bit in a hand- or electric drill.

4.   Finish the head in any creative manner you like. Paint directly on the gourd with water-base paints. For an overall sealer coat, use gesso, as described in the papier-mâché technique, then decorate. You can etch or carve features into the gourd surface, glue protuberances onto it, drill holes and slits to poke in hair, ears, noses, and so forth. A varnish or acrylic medium matte finish may be applied if desirable, but it is not necessary. The finish used will depend solely on the appearance you wish your puppet to have.

Hints for Constructing Puppet Heads and Bodies

Whether you create human or animal puppets, a few construction hints will make your puppets more believable and "alive" looking.

ABOUT HEADS

Think of the head as a rounded form—ball-shaped, egg- or pear-shaped. Sometimes heads are drawn round; but more often the head is longer than it is wide.

Placement and size of the features depend upon the effect you want to achieve. Observe cartoon figures on television and in comic books. Analyze the placement of the features and the changes of expression. The way the eyes and mouth are presented determines the expression of the personality you are creating. Always sketch features on paper before you commit them permanently to a head with paint or markers.

Add noses. Observe placement and types of noses in drawings and in real life to give your puppets character.

BODIES

It is good practice to draw your visualization of a puppet before you begin to create one. Solve your construction problems on paper. Decide how the puppet will be manipulated, how the head will attach to the body, the lengths of arms and legs. Visualize the character in three dimensions, using the basic shapes of circles and ovals for size relationship. Decide how parts of the body will move in relation to one another for the puppet you are developing.

Facial expressions depend on eyes and mouth.

Placement of Features

Ideas for Facial Expressions

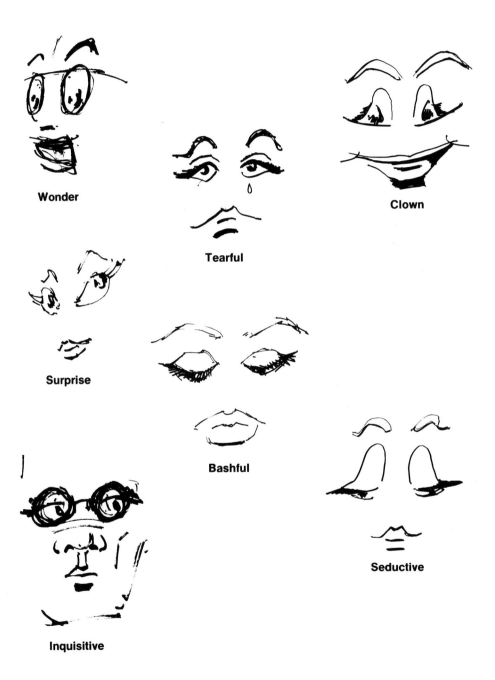

Wonder

Tearful

Clown

Surprise

Bashful

Seductive

Inquisitive

Suggested References

The following is a beginning for ideas for making puppets and using them. Refer to *Books in Print* by subject; and *Books in Print* by title and author at your library. Begin with the listings under "Puppets," "Puppets and Puppet-Plays—History and Criticism," "Fairies," "Clowns," and so forth, depending upon the type of characters you wish to produce.

Also refer to books on drawing faces, caricatures, figures, animation, and so forth. Illustrated children's story books from the United States and foreign countries will also yield inspired characters that can be made in macramé.

Baird, Bil. *Art of the Puppet.* Boston: Plays, Inc., 1966.

Briggs, Katharine M. *Encyclopedia of Fairies: Hobgoblins, Brownies, Bogies, & Other Supernatural Creatures.* New York: Pantheon, 1977.

————. *Encyclopedia of Fairies: Hobgoblins, Brownies, Bogies, & Other Supernatural Creatures.* New York: Pantheon, 1978.

Huygen, Wil. *Gnomes.* New York: Abrams, 1977.

Keene, Donald. *Bunraku: The Art of the Japanese Puppet Theatre.* New York: Kodansha International, Ltd., 1965.

Larkin, David, ed. *Faeries.* New York: Abrams, 1979.

Malkin, Michael R. *Traditional & Folk Puppets of the World.* New York: A. S. Barnes, 1977.

Meilach, Dona Z. *Macramé: Creative Design in Knotting.* New York: Crown Publishers, Inc., 1971.

Muppet Movie Book, The. New York: Abrams, 1979.

Muppet Show Book, The. New York: Abrams, 1979.

Index

C.P. = Color Page

95